POSITIONING THE BRAND

Positioning is hot. Not only in the realm of consumer goods manufacturers, but also for other companies, institutions, governments and even individual people. An explosion of good-quality products on the market and targeted media and advertising campaigns has led to increasing interest from organizations as to how to strategically position their brand.

Up to now, only a few books on positioning have been published. *Positioning the Brand* picks up the gauntlet with an approach based on two fundamental choices: first, the book is written from the perspective of the brand manager, and has therefore been shaped as a practical roadmap. Second, it advocates a new stance on positioning, teaching the reader to look from the inside-out, instead of adopting the usual outside-in methodology. This inside-out approach starts with an analysis of corporate identity, enabling better fulfilment of external positioning and ensuring internal support.

This book is intended for future managers, marketing professionals and communication professionals responsible for the commercial success and reputation of a brand. It has a practical set up, reinforced by engaging examples, and will enable the reader to individually complete a positioning process.

Rik Riezebos is the Managing Director of EURIB/European Institute for Brand Management, the Netherlands, and is the Managing Consultant of Brand Capital, the Netherlands.

Jaap van der Grinten is Lecturer and Research Fellow at Inholland University, the Netherlands.

POSITIONING THE BRAND

An inside-out approach

Rik Riezebos and
Jaap van der Grinten

LONDON AND NEW YORK

First published 2012
by Routledge
2 Park Square, Milton Park, Abingdon, Oxon OX14 4RN

Simultaneously published in the USA and Canada
by Routledge
711 Third Avenue, New York, NY 10017

Routledge is an imprint of the Taylor & Francis Group, an informa business

© 2012 Rik Riezebos and Jaap van der Grinten

The rights of Rik Riezebos and Jaap van der Grinten to be identified
as authors of this work have been asserted by them in accordance with
Sections 77 and 78 of the Copyright, Designs and Patents Act 1988.

All rights reserved. No part of this book may be reprinted or
reproduced or utilised in any form or by any electronic, mechanical,
or other means, now known or hereafter invented, including photocopying
and recording, or in any information storage or retrieval system,
without permission in writing from the publishers.

Trademark notice: Product or corporate names may be trademarks
or registered trademarks, and are used only for identification and
explanation without intent to infringe.

British Library Cataloguing in Publication Data
A catalogue record for this book is available from the British Library

Library of Congress Cataloging in Publication Data
Riezebos, H. J., 1960–.
  Positioning the brand: an inside-out approach/Rik Riezebos and
Jaap van der Grinten.
  p. cm.
  Includes bibliographical references and index.
  1. Product management. 2. Brand name products.
  3. Branding (Marketing). I. Grinten, Jaap van der.
  II. Title.
  HF5415.15.R544 2011
  658.8'27 – dc22   2011013949

ISBN: 978-0-415-66518-6 (hbk)
ISBN: 978-0-415-66519-3 (pbk)
ISBN: 978-0-203-80248-9 (ebk)

Typeset in Bembo and Stone Sans
by Florence Production Ltd, Stoodleigh, Devon

Figure design by Marc van Gijn

Printed and bound in Great Britain by
TJ International Ltd, Padstow, Cornwall

CONTENTS

About the authors — vii
Positioning Roadmap — ix
Preface — xi
Acknowledgements — xiii
Credits — xiv

1 Introduction — 1

1.1 Why position a brand? — 1
1.2 From product to brand — 6
1.3 What is positioning? — 9
1.4 Roadmap — 13

2 Corporate Identity (Step 1) — 18

2.1 Introduction — 19
2.2 History — 21
2.3 Business orientation — 23
2.4 Core competencies — 30
2.5 Vision and mission — 36
2.6 Culture — 41
2.7 Corporate and customer values — 46

3 Brand Architecture (Step 2) — 51

3.1 The three branches of brand architecture — 52
3.2 Brand-name strategy — 53
3.3 Brand portfolio — 59

	3.4 Sub-branding	68
	3.5 Brand architecture conclusions	69

Checklist 1: Summary of the internal analysis — 71

4 Target Group Analysis (Step 3) — 75

	4.1 Mind management	76
	4.2 Means–end analysis	87
	4.3 Conclusions of target group analysis	97

5 Competitor Analysis (Step 4) — 99

	5.1 Competition environment	100
	5.2 Fourteen positioning approaches	102
	5.3 Market exploration in terms of positionings	108

Checklist 2: Summary of the external analysis — 127

6 Choosing a Market Position (Step 5) — 133

	6.1 Reasons for repositioning	133
	6.2 Positioning choice	137
	6.3 Communicative realization	151
	6.4 Closing remarks	165

Appendix A: Brand Key Model	168
Appendix B: Comprehensive list of values	173
Bibliography	177
Index	181
Brand name index	188

ABOUT THE AUTHORS

Dr Rik Riezebos (1960) has been Managing Director of EURIB, the European Institute for Brand Management, since 2002 and is managing consultant at Brand Capital. He studied economic psychology at the University of Tilburg in the Netherlands, followed by a doctorate in General Management from RSM Erasmus University Rotterdam. He went on to join the teaching staff at this faculty in the role of assistant and associate professor in Marketing Communication and Brand Management (1991–2001). In addition to that role, he also held the part-time position of Strategy Director at TBWA/ARA Advertising Agency Consultancy in Rotterdam (1998–2001). Rik Riezebos is the author of the standard work *Brand Management* (2003), which is also available in its original Dutch version and in Chinese.

Jaap van der Grinten MA (1968) teaches brand management, marketing and corporate communication at Inholland University of Applied Sciences in Rotterdam, and is a research fellow at CBRD, the centre for applied research in Cross-media, Brand, Reputation and Design Management, at Inholland. Jaap van der Grinten majored in economics at the University of Groningen, where he later completed the Brand Management postdoc course. After his studies, he held marketing and marketing communication positions at Philips and L'Oréal. He has previously published the book *Mind the Gap* (2004; 2nd edition 2010), a roadmap for identity and image management (in Dutch).

Positioning Roadmap

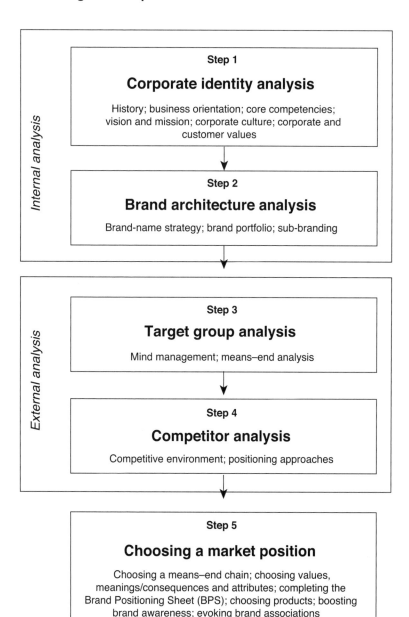

PREFACE

Positioning is a brand management tool that has been attracting increasing levels of interest in recent years. This technique used to be deployed only by providers of consumer goods, but we are now seeing virtually every single company putting serious thought into its brand positioning. Service providers, business-to-business companies, retailers or non-profit organizations, intensive competition is driving all of them to consider raising their market profile. Even small and medium-sized enterprises are turning to brand positioning techniques to help them stand out.

Although positioning is enjoying great popularity in practice, there is still a significant lack of theoretical grounding. In our search for literature on the subject we only encountered a few books. And we also ran up against a second omission: the rare literature on positioning that we did find invariably stresses the choice of a differentiating position in the mind of the target group as the core of positioning. This approach neglects the underlying internal management process that goes into coming up with a positioning that matches the company's identity and circumstances. In this book we have chosen to describe positioning from the perspective of the choice process that a manager has to go through. Our adage is that positioning is all about making choices: choices about what aspects of your product or organization you want to present to the outside world – and which ones you want to emphasize less or perhaps even conceal; choices about who you want as the target group for your brand, and how you want to make your brand meaningful to that target group; and even choices about whom you will consider your competitors, and how your brand can be differentiated from other brands.

This book is set up as a roadmap that provides brand managers with guidance in the making of choices as part of the positioning process. Along the way, we will sometimes take a side-road to go into certain subjects in greater depth to further clarify the context of the steps brand managers have to take. And we would, of course, welcome any comments!

Rik Riezebos and Jaap van der Grinten
Rotterdam/Amstelveen, February 2011
Contact us on info@eurib.org or jvandergrinten@xs4all.nl

Note

This book uses the term 'brand manager' on many occasions. In major organizations, brand management is mostly a role that has been assigned to a specific employee, whereas in smaller organizations it is usually one of the duties of a director or the communication manager. The term 'brand manager' refers to the person responsible for the branding policy of his or her organization, and therefore not necessarily to a specific role.

ACKNOWLEDGEMENTS

We would like to thank a few people for their help in making this book a reality.

As a former lecturer at CBRD, the centre for applied research in Crossmedia, Brand Reputation and Design Management, at Inholland University, Rik Riezebos would like to thank the research fellows of that institute for their unrelenting encouragement to publish this book; especially his co-author Jaap van der Grinten for vivid discussions about the theory and practice of positioning. Further thanks go to Leo van der Blom, Marjolein Kool, Marieke van de Laar, Suzanne Leentvaar, Michiel Noij and Janneke Verhorst of EURIB/European Institute for Brand Management, who let him 'bother' them with numerous questions about literature to consult, cases to include and spelling to use. Gratitude is also due to Harrie Dechering and Albert Top, with whom Rik Riezebos worked on several positioning and brand architecture projects.

Jaap van der Grinten would like to extend his gratitude to his former lecturers Rik Riezebos and Brigitte Wolf at CBRD, as well as the board of the School of Communication and Media of Inholland University for giving him the freedom to develop this book. The following persons deserve special thanks for taking the time to provide feedback on the manuscript: (former) research fellows Helma Weijnand-Schut, Roger Lazenby, Simon Palser, Willy Geurts, Kees van 't Hof, Jos van der Zwaal, Gert Kootstra and Cees van Wijk, associate lecturer at CBRD. Special thanks also go to Marieke van de Pol for permission to use the resources of the FHV/BBDO research institute. And last, but not least, he is most grateful to all students and lecturers of the Brand Management course for their enthusiasm and tips, and would like to single out lecturers Bram Padmos, Mylène van Veldhoven and Roger Lazenby for special thanks.

Finally, both Rik Riezebos and Jaap van der Grinten would like to thank Erwin Postma for translating the original Dutch text into English, and for helping the authors to find international cases.

CREDITS

Chapter 1

Box 1.1: Bonne Maman logo used with permission of Andros France S.N.C.
Box 1.2: Blog text used with permission of Guardian News & Media Ltd.

Chapter 2

Box 2.1: Océ logo and picture of Karel and Louis van der Grinten used with permission of Océ-Technologies B.V.
Box 2.2: Salanova logo and picture used with permission of RijkZwaan B.V.
Box 2.3: Virgin logo used with permission of Virgin Management Ltd.
Box 2.6: Picture ID&T Sensations used with permission of Rutger Geerling.
Box 2.8: Marlies Dekkers logo used with permission of md design & communication B.V.
Table 2.3: Adapted from Cameron, K.S. and Quinn, R.E. (2006), revised edition. Copyright © 2006 by John Wiley & Sons, Inc., used with permission of John Wiley & Sons, Inc.

Chapter 3

Box 3.1: Unilever logo used with permission of Unilever Nederland B.V.
Pictures Mona, Vifit, Optimel used with permission of Koninklijke FrieslandCampina N.V.
Nivea Visage, Nivea for Men and Nivea Sun logos used with permission of Beiersdorf AG.

Chapter 4

Picture of BMW C1 used with permission of BMW Group/Motorrad.
Figure 4.6: Adapted from Olson, J.C. and Reynolds, T.J. (1983), in Percy, L. and Woodside, A (1983 p. 77–90), copyright © 1983 Lexington Books. Used with permission of Lexington Books.
Figure 4.7: Adapted from Reynolds, T.J. and Gutman, J. (2001), in Reynolds T.J. and Olson, J.C. (2001, p. 27), copyright © Taylor and Francis Group LLC. Used with permission of Taylor and Francis Group LLC.

Chapter 5

Box 5.1: TomTom logo used with permission of TomTom International B.V.
Picture of Bacardi party used with permission of Ed Hicks.
Picture of Amsterdam card used with permission of Amsterdam Toerisme en Congres Bureau. Picture Oslo Pass used with permission of VisitOSLO.

Chapter 6

Box 6.5: Omo logo used with permission of Unilever Nederland B.V.
Box 6.6: Logos Shell Pura, Shell V-Power and Shell FuellSave used with permission of Shell Nederland B.V.
Table 6.2: Adapted from Rossiter, J.R. and Bellman, S. (2005), copyright © 2005 Pearson Plc. Used with permission of Pearson Plc.

Appendix B

Reprinted from Franzen, G., Goessens, C., Hoogerbrugge, M., Kappert, C., Schuring, R.J., Vogel, M. (1998), copyright © 1998 Giep Franzen. Used with permission of Giep Franzen.

1
INTRODUCTION

Positioning is a marketing tool that has been attracting increasing levels of interest in recent years. In this book we will present a roadmap for a brand positioning process following an inside-out approach.[1] This first chapter will focus on a number of basic questions about positioning, such as why positioning is relevant for companies and institutions (Section 1.1). The rapid rise of positioning is partly due to the development of numerous ideas on brands and brand policy. Section 1.2 therefore goes on to outline the shift from the product-driven to the brand-driven approach in marketing. Section 1.3 subsequently defines positioning, focusing on some important aspects. Section 1.4 concludes the chapter and opens up the structure of the rest of the book through the 'positioning roadmap'.

1.1 Why position a brand?

In this first section we will look into why positioning is important. After a brief introduction, we will outline three developments that have increased the importance of positioning to companies:

1. The increase in the number of available products and services (the so-called *product explosion*).[2]
2. The visibility of the organizations behind products and services has increased in importance (in this book we have labelled this the *organization explosion*);
3. The huge growth of media and advertising outlets (the so-called *media explosion*).

2 Introduction

A good product sells itself...?

'A good product sells itself.' That used to be a much-heard phrase in marketing circles. In the second half of the 20th century, product quality (of both goods and services) largely levelled out. Sure, there are still differences in quality between products, but the major differences of 20 or 30 years ago have all but disappeared.[3] The above adage therefore now implies that virtually every single product will sell itself these days, meaning that consumers now face the task of choosing from an overwhelming offering of quality goods and services. In turn, this means that every single provider has to put some serious thought into the question of how to make his product stand out in comparison to those of his competitors. In marketing terms this is referred to as *brand positioning*. This requires that a manager must answer two key questions:

1. What are the associations that the brand must evoke in the target group?
2. How can the brand be differentiated from its competitors?

Effective positioning ensures that a brand attracts the attention of customers, and that the associations evoked by the communication are sufficiently relevant to get people to buy the brand product. We have therefore opted to replace the old adage of 'a good product sells itself' by the principle that 'a good product deserves a good positioning'.

In practice, positioning often fails to take into account whether actual choices were made. This is one of the major dilemmas: when making a clear choice for one positioning, the danger seems to be that you are excluding certain target groups or limiting the scope of consumption. A great number of managers will therefore choose a positioning that presents the brand as a jack-of-all-trades offering something for everyone – despite the ample proof provided by various success stories that clear targeting in positioning does indeed yield good results.[4] Marlboro, for example, was at one point positioned as a cigarette brand for men, but also turned out to be quite popular with women. The leading mint chocolate brand After Eight is successfully positioned as an after-dinner mint. Of course this positioning will not prevent consumers enjoying After Eight at other times of the day. Another good example of 'targeted' positioning is the American town of Clute, Texas. This town is known for its annual mosquito plague. In 2011, Clute celebrated the 31st annual Mosquito Festival, a three-day event attracting over 15,000 tourists! This example shows that even positioning on the basis of negative aspects can work, as long as it is targeted.[5]

We have provided a number of general reasons behind the importance of adequately positioning a product in the market. Three key changes have led to the present situation where a product is doomed to fail in the market without a sophisticated positioning strategy. We will go further into these changes in the following sections on the product, organization and media explosions.

Product explosion

The number of products and services on offer has seen a huge rise in recent years. Just take a look at the breakfast cereal aisle at any large supermarket, where you will find an extensive offering of cereal options. New combinations (Special K Chocolatey Delight), new box sizes (single-serve box), new shapes (especially those targeting children) and new categories (cereal bars and low-fat cereals), to name but a few. Even buying a loaf of bread nowadays requires us to choose from a wide range of different products. The old-fashioned white loaf has been joined by brown, wholemeal, multigrain, organic, thick-sliced, thin-sliced, weekender and malted brown loafs on local bakers' shelves or in supermarkets' bread aisles, not to mention the ciabattas, naans, daktylas, focaccias, French sticks, etc. that cater to shoppers looking for an international bread sensation. Virtually every conceivable market has seen a product explosion. And these product explosions have led not only to the availability of more product versions, but also to the linking of certain services to physical products – such as car manufacturers setting up their own banks for financing and leasing (for example BMW group financial and Groupe RCI Banque, which offers financial services to Renault, Nissan and Dacia). All these cases show that the enormous offering of similar quality products has made it increasingly difficult for a provider of branded products to stand out and curry favour with consumers. Positioning is a mode of thought and a method to cope with this issue.

Where the product explosion is concerned, it should be borne in mind that many markets have seen an enormous growth in the number of products on offer coupled with strong reductions in the differences in quality between them. Services in particular are proving easy to copy by competitors; an insurance policy, for example, can literally be copied by a competitor – by simply photocopying it. But unique and relevant positioning is a lot harder to copy.

Organization explosion

In discussing the product explosion above we referred to the goods and services offered by companies or organizations. Up to the early 1990s, many of these organizations were hardly, or not at all, visible to the public. Consumers were aware of the name of the organization behind the product only if the product brand name was the same as the name of the organization, such as in the case of many Asian brands, such as Samsung and Sony. Company names like Procter & Gamble, Benckiser and Sara Lee were rarely, if ever, used in the external communication of those companies. In most European countries it was not even possible to register a company name as a brand name until the 1980s.

From the early 1990s, increasing numbers of organizations started developing an awareness that they should present themselves more to the outside world as 'the company behind the brand'.[6] This movement was partly down to the fact that other stakeholder groups (i.e. not customers) and other subjects were becoming more important for the continuity of the organization. For example:

- The war for talent on the labour market meant that companies had to put greater effort into building their reputation on the labour market than before.
- There was increasing pressure to be accountable in terms of the company's corporate social responsibility.
- Shareholder power became greater.

The increasing interest in corporate brands has also been fuelled by the publication of all kinds of company rankings. The American Fortune 500 list, for example, is based on companies' gross revenue, whereas the *Financial Times'* EMRC (Europe's Most Respected Companies) ranks companies on reputation, and the 'Great Place to Work' ranking looks at factors such as working environment and the extent to which companies are good employers. All these phenomena have contributed to what in this book we refer to as the 'organization explosion'. That does not point at a growing number of organizations, but rather at the greater *presence* and *visibility* of existing organizations. This greater degree of visibility is mainly a result of companies feeling a stronger need to stand out than they used to.

Media explosion

Alongside a product explosion and an organization explosion, the last two decades have also seen a 'media explosion'. Over the past decade commercial TV has found its way throughout Europe and dramatically changed the media landscape by multiplying the number of available channels. We have so many more TV channels, radio stations and magazines to choose from than we did 20 years ago. And that also means a corresponding surge in advertising. Even public life is littered with advertising on billboards, bus shelters, sandwich boards, megaboards, cars, lorries, buses, trams, trains, taxis, bikes, boats, and even pedal boats. And digitalization has brought all this advertising to the Internet and our mobile phones as well. The amount of information available directly on the Internet is dazzling, and only getting more immense. The media explosion has made it harder for providers to get through to consumers. This has, in turn, heralded the downfall of several second- and third-rate brands. Companies that want to continue to get their message across to consumers through the media are feeling the pinch of a considerable hike in expenses. One astute manager at Procter & Gamble calculated that in 1970, 70 per cent of the target group in the market could be reached by airing 13 TV ads, whereas that range would now require 135 (!) ads. That makes positioning and/or communication blunders very costly.

Therefore: positioning

Positioning is the prime method to counter the effects of the product, organization and media explosions. By choosing a differentiating positioning that is relevant to the target group, a product brand or corporate brand can stand out amidst the huge offering of other brands and the overkill of media and advertising campaigns. Formulating a well-founded positioning creates a framework that makes the right choices in terms of product offering and message apparent. The chance of success is hence increased to a considerable extent. To further substantiate this, Box 1.1 describes the case of a product brand, Bonne Maman. Bonne Maman is a company that has managed to claim a unique position in the jam market by marketing its products in a way that is different, but very relevant to consumers.

In our opinion, the unique thing about Bonne Maman is the way it positions its products in the market. The naming and presentation of the product in a container that looks like the improvised containers people use when making jam at home stress the 'authenticity' and 'purity' of the product. Bonne Maman has chosen a positioning that is carried through in all aspects of the brand product. This success came from within the company. The company was good at making conserves using traditional methods. That core competency was extended to biscuits and tarts in a recognizable way. There is nothing wrong with positioning a brand along very sharp lines, which some managers may even consider too narrow; Bonne Maman clearly proves that.

BOX 1.1 THE HOMEMADE FEEL OF BONNE MAMAN JAM

Today almost everyone recognizes Bonne Maman jam through the instant appeal of its packaging. The chunky ribbed glass jar, with red and white gingham print lid and 'handwritten' name on the label, give it an unmistakably authentic look and feel. Made from pure ingredients and seemingly using the same recipes as our mothers and grandmothers used for their homemade jams, it brings back warm memories of our childhood (notwithstanding the fact that Bonne Maman products are in fact produced industrially). This strong association with authenticity has led Bonne Maman to successfully extend its product range to yoghurts, desserts, tarts and biscuits.

Positioning is a technique that emerged when managers started abandoning the age-old adage of a good product – or organization – selling itself. They started to realize that the image created around the product or the organization also plays a key role. The fact that herds of managers have come round to the relevance of positioning is linked to the advent of the 'brand-driven approach'. The following section will go into the shift from a product-driven to a brand-driven approach in marketing.

1.2 From product to brand

This book focuses on *brand* positioning. This section will explain the difference between a product and a brand.

Product

Most people identify a product with a tangible object. But this book uses a wider definition of product to include both goods and services. Products are therefore not only goods such as peanut butter, cars or computers, but also services, such as insurances and holidays. Even the promises made by a political party can be considered a product. By approaching services as a product, a string of top chefs realized they had great potential to be very successful in the marketing of cooking-related items. One such mediagenic gastronome is Jamie Oliver, the restaurant chef turned TV chef, cookery book writer, health campaigner, culinary educator, and ultimately celebrity chef. 'Jamie Oliver' is a brand name, because it adds value to the products that come with the Jamie Oliver stamp (see Box 1.2).

Brand

Most markets are these days filled with products that are almost all of good quality, and by organizations that never pass up on an opportunity to stress their corporate social responsibility. Many products and organizations

---

BOX 1.2 THE JAMIE OLIVER BRAND[7]

On 13 September 2006, Jamie Oliver appeared in his 100th advertisement for Sainsbury's since signing on as the face of the supermarket back in 2000. He has proved to have a Teflon image, hardly putting a foot wrong. His TV chef-turned-health campaign image has indirectly proved a free-advertising bonanza for Sainsbury's.

It could be argued that it was the 2002 launch of the Jamie's School Dinners show and subsequent re-invention of Oliver as a People's Champion that stopped a backlash against what at the time was threatening to become cheeky-chappy overkill. As Patrick Smity, European Chief Executive of FutureBrand, argues: 'His personal brand is in the ascendancy and he has gone beyond celebrity chef to deal with major health and diet issues. He personifies the brand. And hats off to any man that can cause a 290 per cent surge in the sales of asparagus.' In 2011, after 11 years, Jamie Oliver ended his partnership with Sainsbury's to spend more time on social projects through his Jamie Oliver Foundation.

Jamie Oliver was born in May 1975 and grew up in Clavering, Essex, where his father runs a pub–restaurant, 'The Cricketers'. He left school at 16 and went to Westminster Catering College, after which he spent time in France, worked with Antonio Carluccio, and went on to work at the highly acclaimed River Café. He featured in a TV documentary about the River Café, which aired in 1997. The day after the broadcast, Jamie was contacted by five TV production companies; the Naked Chef was born! The Jamie Oliver brand currently features on nine books and sells a wide range of products under the 'Jme' sub-brand, such as kitchenware, an outdoor collection, a food range, herbs, scented candles, DVDs, and even a cooking game for Nintendo DS consoles.

therefore meet the expectations and requirements of their target groups. This makes it quite hard for a provider or organization to differentiate themselves from their competitors. Approaching a product or organization as a brand can offer a way out of this deadlock. The difference between a product and a brand was once phrased as follows: 'A product is manufactured in a factory, while a brand only exists in the consumer's mind.' Although this statement considers product and consumer good to be the same thing, it does pinpoint the essential difference between a product and a brand. But it still falls short, because it does not answer the question of how to turn a product or an organization into a brand. To answer that question, you need to bear in mind that there is one principal difference between a brand and a product or organization: a brand has a unique, and hence differentiating, brand name. Take the yoghurts market, where a string of different brands vie for consumers' attention. If one brand claims to make the best-tasting yoghurts, it will be hard for a consumer to choose when faced with a supermarket shelf stacked with (unbranded) yoghurt products. But on the basis of a brand name one can identify a specific product. An additional advantage is that consumers have certain associations with a brand name, and can come to believe that this specific branded product is better than the same product made by other companies. A brand allows the provider to give his products a place in the minds of the people in his target group, and hence differentiate his products. An organization can also claim differentiating associations through a brand.

The concept 'brand' has many different definitions. It is important to bear in mind that there are two relevant views of the concept 'brand'. On the one hand, a brand can be taken as an observable name or logo. This normally means referring to a brand as a (visible) *sign*. We are then dealing with the physical appearance of a brand. For Alfa Romeo, for example, this is the brand name and its characteristic logo (which combines two symbols of the city of Milan: the Visconti family snake symbol and a red cross against a white background). For the corporate brand Unilever, the physical brand appearance is the capital 'U', made up of 25 symbols representing different aspects of the company (see Chapter 3). On the other hand, a brand can be interpreted as a mental representation in the mind of the consumer. In the case of Alfa Romeo this consists of the associations that consumers have with that brand, such as Italy, fast cars and beautiful design. And in Unilever's case these would be associations along the lines of an Anglo-Dutch company with fine brands and good career opportunities. We have conceived the following definition to stress both brand views:[8]

A brand is a sign (name and/or logo) with the power to differentiate the goods or services of a company – or the organization itself – and represents a certain meaning to the target group in either a material or an immaterial sense.

It is indeed useful to distinguish between a product and a brand, because the members of a target group link certain associations to a brand in their minds, which makes them believe that the product in question is better than those of competing brands, or that the organization in question has more to offer them than other organizations.

Nowadays, brands are more important in our thought patterns than products or organizations. This is due to the following reasons:

- It is still often hard to set products apart from each other.
- A brand can claim all kinds of advantageous features and emotions a customer can link to a name that is unique to that brand.
- In the profusion of choice that we are now seeing, a brand acts as a 'guide'.
- Apart from discernability, people need confidence, appreciation, status, and a feeling of taking good care of themselves.

Take Nike. Nike has long ceased to be a mere name of trainers, and has become a super brand that is highly charged with emotional values. The brand name Nike is therefore currently used to sell all sorts of products in many different categories. The brand has taken centre stage, and the different products give that brand its meaning.

To conclude this section, we will focus on the difference between two 'archetypical brands': Coca-Cola and Pepsi-Cola. Box 1.3 outlines the history of these brands, highlighting the differences. This cola case will go to show that the brand is indeed more important than the product, and that the differences in the experience of both brand products are literally based on the different places these brands occupy in our minds. Section 1.3 will further delve into the question of what positioning entails. It will, furthermore, provide a definition of this concept.

1.3 What is positioning?

In this section we will further define *positioning*, and delve into the three key elements of our definition. Our definition of positioning is as follows:

Positioning entails a brand manager making a well-considered choice of which aspects of the brand identity must be emphasized. The chosen aspects have to be relevant to the (potential) target group and differentiate the brand from competing brands.

BOX 1.3 COCA-COLA VERSUS PEPSI-COLA[9]

Coca-Cola was invented by John Pemberton, a pharmacist, who first sold this brand product in Atlanta, Georgia, in 1886, at 5 cents a glass. Within three weeks of the introduction of Coca-Cola, The Atlanta Daily published the first advertisement with the heading 'Coca-Cola. Delicious! Refreshing! Exhilarating! Invigorating!' Shortly before his death in 1888, Pemberton sold the concept for $1200 to Asa G. Chandler, who went on to set up The Coca-Cola Company in 1892 (a company that currently exploits more than 400 different brands). The name Coca-Cola supposedly referred to the ingredients that were used to make this refreshing beverage: coca leaf and cola nut extracts. The shortened version of the name, Coke, was officially registered as a brand name alongside Coca-Cola in 1945.

The man behind Pepsi-Cola (1898) was Caleb Bradham, a pharmacist from New Bern (North Carolina). He initially intended Pepsi-Cola as an elixir to combat dyspepsia, a kind of indigestion consisting of pain or an uncomfortable feeling in the abdomen after eating a meal. Bradham's company went bankrupt in 1923, and the properties and brand name were bought by the Loft Candy Company. This company managed to carve out a spot in the market for Pepsi-Cola by selling it cheaply and in recycled beer bottles. In those days, Pepsi was considered a poor man's soft drink.

In the second half of the 20th century, Coca-Cola and Pepsi-Cola were locked in a continuous battle. During the 1980s, Pepsi attempted to convince consumers that Pepsi tasted better than Coca-Cola. The 'Pepsi Challenge' saw consumers at shopping malls asked to try both soft drinks and express a preference. It was a so-called 'blind test', with both colas only denoted by a single letter ('M' for Pepsi-Cola and 'Q' for Coca-Cola). These tests showed that consumers preferred Pepsi-Cola. Criticism of the Pepsi Challenge pointed out that the preference for Pepsi can largely be attributed to the letters that were used. Seeing as the letter

continued . . .

Q is less common in our day-to-day language use than the letter M, people are drawn more easily to the latter.

Nowadays, MRI scans allow us to look inside people's heads. Read Montague, an American scientist, used this technology and found that the brands Coca-Cola and Pepsi-Cola are stored in different sections in the consumer's brain, and therefore literally have a different mind share (Figure 1.1). Montague found that when consumers were told they were drinking Coca-Cola, three-quarters of them suddenly said the cola tasted better, which is down to the fact that another part of their brain was activated. The mere mention of the name Coca-Cola activated the medial prefrontal cortex, a part of the brain where higher cognitive processes are located. Montague concluded that the brain activates certain information that was input by advertising upon hearing the name Coca-Cola, and that these associations are so powerful that they influence our objective observation (of taste).

In the present-day soft drinks market, Coca-Cola trumps Pepsi-Cola almost everywhere in the world. In 2008, Coca-Cola's market share in the USA was estimated at 42.7 per cent, against Pepsi-Cola's 30.8 per cent. In 2010, the international branding consultancy Interbrand valued the Coca-Cola brand at $70.5 billion and the Pepsi-Cola brand at $14.1 billion (a factor of 5 difference).

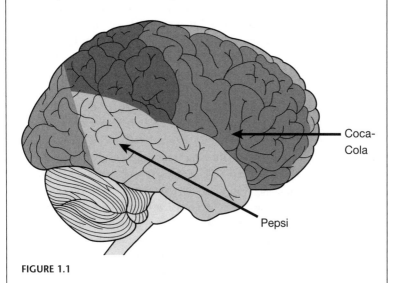

FIGURE 1.1

Other definitions mainly highlight the desired mind share in the receivers of the brand communication. By bringing the brand manager's choice process to the fore, our definition better dovetails with the way companies organize positioning processes in practice. Furthermore, this definition stresses that you should first take a good look at your own identity (what can you deliver on, and what not?), and that you should not be led by the consumer too much during the positioning process. Literature on this subject refers to the latter danger as the 'image trap'.[10] The outcome of the positioning process will, of course, have to be that the desired set of associations surrounding the brand name is created in the mind of the receiver.

In the above definition we present positioning as a 'well-considered choice'. This idea of a well-considered choice is twofold: 'well-considered' and 'choice'. *Well-considered* means that positioning involves you, as the brand manager, making a choice that you have thought long and hard about. The chosen market position will then be a lasting one, and not be replaced by another at the slightest setback. Although it is impossible to provide any general guidelines for the duration of a positioning, a well-substantiated and well-founded positioning should hold for at least three to four years. It would in any case always be a good idea to consider repositioning a brand after that period of time has passed.

The second component of 'well-considered choice' implies that you, the brand manager, will make a *choice*. The brand manager has to choose which aspects of the identity to emphasize, and which ones the manager does not want to emphasize (i.e. which associations the manager wants the brand to evoke). Several considerations enter into this choice process. First of all, the product category of the brand product has to be identified, as well as the reasons for buying the product that matter, or could matter, to the target group. Based on this information, the manager will have to define what the positioning has to emphasize in order to latch onto the product class, *the points of parity*, and which associations can differentiate the brand in question from those of its competitors, *the points of difference*. The latter requires a manager to be up to speed on the needs of the target group, as well as on the motivations engendering these needs. A training centre, for example, can come to the conclusion that people sign up for a vocational course on the basis of two different motivations: to boost career prospects by obtaining a diploma in the field in question, or to take the course as a kind of 'intellectual challenge'.

Another important consideration when choosing the associations that you wish the brand to conjure up is the question whether these match the identity of the organization. Volvo, for example, has in recent years been harping on about safety, but in April 2011 Renault had more models in its line with the highest EURONCAP safety rating than Volvo did.[11] Although this does not mean Volvo cannot claim the concept 'safety', it does mean Volvo has to go all out in the near future to launch more models with the highest EURONCAP safety rating. And lastly, choosing the desired association could lead you to note that the chosen positioning should fit in with the existing positionings for other brand products within the organization.

At this stage we would like to stress once again that, as a brand manager, you really have to make a choice. Customers will mostly instinctively choose the best option for them. They are therefore looking for specialist brands that they can clearly tell excel. Or, in the words of a famous advertising guru: 'If you try to be everything to everybody, you end up being nothing to nobody.' The choice process often proves tough going. By not only defining who you will cater to, but also defining who you will not cater to, you are setting the boundaries for targeted positioning. To many entrepreneurs this will feel as if they are letting revenue-generating opportunities slip. However, when generating some revenue in several target groups, while competitors are taking the lion's share in each specific target group time and again, all these 'little shares' will in time start to feel the heat. A strong position with one specific group is easier to defend than a weak position with many different groups.

This section has defined what positioning is all about. We have provided and explained our definition of this concept, as well as a number of relevant aspects of positioning. To wrap up this chapter, we present a roadmap that includes all steps on the way to powerful positioning. Each of these steps will be further detailed separately in the following chapters.

1.4 Roadmap

As a brand manager, you have to make some key choices to position your brand. Key choices are what needs your positioning will target, while the brand product will actually tailor to more, and the choice of a clearly defined target group.

The roadmap presented in this book will help you make all the choices that lead to effective and targeted positioning. We will guide you on the basis of the BTC model, which stands for 'Brand–Target Group–Competitors'. Figure 1.2 depicts these three variables in three homonymic circles. The 'Brand' circle stresses analysis of the so-called internal environment of the brand in question. The term 'internal environment' refers to the characteristics of the organization engendering the brand. This internal analysis consists of two parts: the analysis of the 'corporate identity' and the analysis of 'brand architecture'. The 'Target group' circle is all about the analysis of the brand's

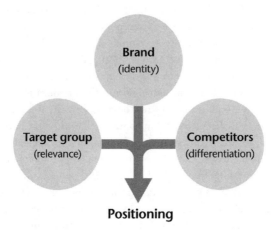

FIGURE 1.2 The BTC model for positioning

target group (such as customers or potential employees). And the 'Competitors' circle contains the analysis of the brand's competitors. Only after mapping all this information can you make a well-founded choice for your brand's positioning. In the following we will briefly explain the BTC model using the five steps from the positioning roadmap.

Steps 1 and 2: Analyse the internal environment (brand identity)

Step 1: The corporate identity

Chapter 2 deals with the first stage of the positioning roadmap: analysing the corporate identity. Before starting to think about what positioning to choose for a brand, it is helpful to get to the bottom of what the organization producing the brand product is all about. A 'me-too positioning' for a brand will, for example, not be in keeping with the image of an innovation-driven organization. When analysing the identity of the organization, we will, among other things, consider the organization's history and its core competencies.

Step 2: Brand architecture

In Chapter 3, we will take a close look at the second stage of the roadmap. This includes investigating how the brand in question relates – or should relate – to the organization's other brands. These can be other product brands, but harmonization with the corporate brand is also called for here. Volkswagen Group, for example, has had to tweak the positioning of its four main brands – VW, Audi, Seat and Škoda – in recent years, because these were all appealing to the same consumer motivations for purchase.

Following Chapter 3, we have included a checklist relating to the brand's internal environment. This checklist lists the key points of the corporate identity (Chapter 2) and the brand architecture (Chapter 3). Completing this checklist will paint a clear picture of the background of the brand that you are positioning.

Steps 3 and 4: Analyse the external environment (target group and competitors)

Step 3: Target group

Chapter 4 goes into the brand's target group. Insight into the mind of the customer is the key to successful positioning. This chapter also reserves ample space for a method of analysis you can use to find out which product offering best fills the needs of a target group. What is important to the target group, and – more importantly – why?

Step 4: Competitors

In Chapter 5, we will focus on the analysis of the competition. This includes a classification of a market and the brands operating in that market into 14 different positioning categories. Based on these categories, you can identify the points on which a brand can still stand out in that market.

Chapter 5 is followed by a second checklist, which relates to the brand's external environment (customer and competitors). After completing this checklist and the one for the internal environment, you, as the brand manager, will have completed the analysis part of the roadmap. It will then prove a lot easier to make choices for the brand's new positioning.

Step 5: Positioning

After having gathered all relevant information in steps 1–4, step 5 (Chapter 6) will consist of defining the final positioning. At this stage, you will have to decide what to emphasize and why. The significance of the brand product to the target group is of leading importance here. A central component of this chapter is the 'Brand Positioning Sheet', a model that summarizes the positioning. This chapter also includes pointers on how all of this can be reflected in and converted into (marketing) communication, among other things.

Note to the reader

Until recently, brand positioning has mainly been described and applied using an outside-in approach. That meant that the external environment was used as the starting point when selecting a brand positioning strategy. This approach often works particularly well for product brands that are sold through the supermarket channel. But nowadays, most brand positioning happens at service providers, on the level of organization brands, in business-to-business markets, and at small and medium-sized enterprises. At all these kinds of companies, employee behaviour has a key role in getting the brand positioning across and building a brand image. Service providers and organization brands have seen the boundaries between internal and external fade. The people behind the brand make the brand. This reality curtails the leverage for authentic positioning of service and organization brands in comparison with product brands, where a brand promise can be 'created' to a greater degree.[12] As a result of continued use of the outside-in approach, many chosen brand positions fail as the brand turns out to be incapable of structurally living up to the brand promise. We have therefore chosen to have the analysis of the brand's own identity precede the analysis of the target group and competitors (inside-out). This implies that self-knowledge is a key basis for success. Finding a good match between brand and target group is, after all, the first step on the road to success. This approach is reflected in the BTC model described above, which starts off by analysing the organization identity. The Brand Positioning Sheet that is used to recap the selected brand positioning in Chapter 6 also adopts the inside-out approach. And for all those readers who are responsible for a product brand that would benefit more from an outside-in brand positioning approach, we have included the Brand Key Model in Appendix A. This model is based on traditional outside-in thinking and methods.

Notes

1 See de Wit and Meyer (2005, Chapter 5) on the paradox of markets and resources, which reflect the outside-in (markets) and inside-out (resources) approach.
2 See Ries and Trout (2001, pp. 16–17).

Introduction 17

3 The degree to which consumers perceive branded products to be similar is usually referred to as *brand parity*. A study by BBDO Worldwide on brand parity in various product classes showed that brand parity was lowest for cigarettes (52 per cent), followed by beer, coffee, shampoo, TV sets, personal computers, airline companies, soap tablets, colas, snacks, dry packed soups and paper towels, and was highest for credit cards (76 per cent). Source: 'Focus: a world of brand parity', a study published by BBDO Worldwide (1988). See also Aaker (1991, p. 10).
4 Both (1992) reports upon a study regarding the performance of consumer product brand image strategies in global markets. The results show that companies that employ a depth strategy (i.e. a clear targeting in positioning) yield a better performance than companies that follow a breadth brand image strategy. See also Rossiter and Percy (1997, p.148).
5 Source: www.mosquitofestival.com (accessed 20 September 2010).
6 See King (1991), Ind (1997), Kapferer (2001, Chapter 2) and Knox (2004).
7 Excerpts from the article 'Does the brand Jamie Oliver have a shelf-life?', posted by Mark Sweney on www.guardian.co.uk, 14 September 2006. Source: www.guardian.co.uk/media/organgrinder/2006/sep/14/doesbrandjamieoliverhavea (accessed 20 September 2010).
8 Based on a definition given by Riezebos (2003).
9 Sources: Wikipedia; McClure *et al.* (2004); *Beverage Digest* 2009, vol. 54, no. 7; Interbrand report *Best Global Brands 2010*. Source: www.interbrand.com (accessed 27 September 2010).
10 See Aaker (1996, pp. 69–70).
11 When looking purely at the safety of adult passengers, in April 2011 Renault had nine models with the highest five-star rating (Clio, Espace, Koleos, Laguna, Megane, Megane CC, Modus, Scenic and Vel Satis) and two with a four-star rating (Kangoo and Twingo). Volvo, on the other hand, had five models with a five-star rating (C30, S40, V70, XC60 and XC90) and three with a four-star rating (S60, S70 and S80). In other words, 82 per cent of the Renault models had the highest five-star rating, whereas 'only' 63 per cent of the Volvo models had been given this rating. Source: www.euroncap.com (accessed 7 April 2011).
12 Kapferer (2008, pp. 28–29).

2

CORPORATE IDENTITY (STEP 1)

This book presents a roadmap for the positioning of a brand following the inside-out approach. One of the first questions a brand manager has to answer in a brand positioning process is what the nature of the organization producing the brand is. This chapter will therefore focus on the characteristics of the organization behind the brand that is supposed to be positioned (a corporate or a product brand). We will do so by delving into the six aspects of corporate identity, which include core competencies, corporate culture, and the values pursued within and by the organization. By getting to the bottom of the organization's identity, we will gain insight into what the playing field will be for the brand. The organization will, after all, have to be able to live up to the positioning that is eventually chosen. That makes knowledge of the organization's strengths and weaknesses key.

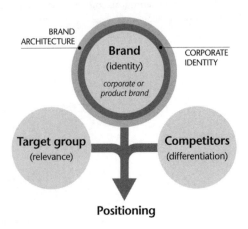

FIGURE 2.1 Corporate identity as part of the internal analysis of the positioning process

Figure 2.1 further fleshes out the BTC model. The top circle is now lined by two additional layers around the brand we are positioning: corporate identity (the essential characteristics of the organization generating the brand) and the brand architecture of this organization. Before making any positioning decisions, you should check not only whether a certain positioning is in keeping with the identity of the organization in question, but also to what extent it tallies with the positioning of other brands from the same organization's portfolio. Chapter 3 will go further into the issue of brand architecture. In the present chapter we will first enter into the six aspects of corporate identity.

2.1 Introduction

Before pursuing the internal analysis of the organization further, we will first briefly explain the difference between the two types of brands: a corporate brand and a product brand. A brand can be classified as a *corporate brand* when the name of the organization (holding or subsidiary) is used as the brand name on products (such as Philips or Yamaha). A *product brand*, on the other hand, is a brand name that is specific to a product produced by an organization.[1] Some organizations use only their corporate brand, others only product brands, and yet others use both their corporate brand and product brands. An example of an organization that uses both its corporate brand and several product brands is TUI: this is a corporate brand in the travel industry (TUI travel agencies in Germany, TUIfly airline, etc.), but it also uses product brands such as First Choice Holidays, Thomson Holidays and Lunn Poly.

A brand that needs to be positioned in the market can be either a corporate brand or a product brand. With both types of brands it is necessary to take a closer look at the defining features of the organization behind the brand before you can actually start positioning the brand. It may seem more pressing to review the organization behind the brand in the case of a corporate brand than in the case of a product brand, since a corporate brand basically represents the organization.[2] However, it is equally important for product brands to take the corporate identity into consideration when deciding on brand positioning issues. Although it is not always clear what organization lies behind a product brand, the organization will always – consciously or subconsciously – leave its mark on the product brand or the way this product brand is presented in advertising. Procter & Gamble provides a good example of the latter. This manufacturer of fast-moving consumer goods is very keen to market product brands with specific features (for example, brands such as Head & Shoulders, Always and Pringles). The identity of the organization is clearly reflected in the positioning of different product brands. Brand positioning (of either a corporate brand or product brand) therefore requires sound knowledge of the identity of the organization behind the brand.

The following six factors add up to the corporate identity (see Figure 2.2):

- The organization's history: an organization's history can tell us a lot about its identity. It is useful to know the founding principles of an organization, and have an idea of the milestones in its history (for example, a crisis or cross-border expansion).
- Business orientation: in most organizations, the management focus will be on one or two of the following four aspects: product quality, process management, raising the external profile, or collaboration. It is important in a positioning process to know what this focus is on.
- Core competencies: an organization's raison d'être is often based on something it is good at — its core competencies. When positioning a brand, it is crucial to have a clear idea of what the organization behind the brand masters better than its competitors.
- Vision and mission: how do people within the organization see the market in the future (vision) and what (growth) objectives have been formulated for the company (mission)?

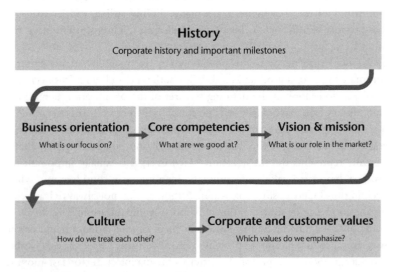

FIGURE 2.2 Six aspects of corporate identity

- Culture: how can the corporate culture of the organization in question be described, and how do people treat each other within the company?
- Corporate and customer values: what values is the organization pursuing internally, and which ones is it looking to present to customers?

Business orientation, core competencies, and vision and mission are all aspects of strategic management, and are usually defined by the management of an organization. Culture and corporate and customer values are aspects that come under the responsibilities of human resources management (HRM) and (internal) communication. The following six sections will further flesh out the above aspects of corporate identity. Bear in mind that these six factors are closely interlinked. We will illustrate this connection using a model that distinguishes four types of organizations. This model will be introduced in Section 2.3.

2.2 History

A corporate identity springs from an organization's history and background. Answering the following questions will help you map your organization's history:

- How did we come about?
- Where do we come from?
- Who are our founders and what where the founding principles?
- What myths and stories have been passed on from our past?
- What important milestones can we identify in the organization's history?

In Box 2.1 we illustrate how an organization's history underpins its identity by way of the example of Océ (incorporated by Canon in 2010). Océ's history tells us quite a lot about the company's identity. One of the main conclusions we can draw is that research and development (R&D) is a key focus at Océ. At Océ innovators are continuously working on coming up with new high-quality solutions, while customers are not always in the market for the technologically most advanced product. Every now and then, Océ struggles with this dilemma: its predilection for research often clashes with the need to tailor to the customer's needs and wishes as best as possible. This results in a clear cultural difference between the operating companies (OPCOs), which maintain customer contacts, and the head office, where the R&D department is based.

BOX 2.1 OCÉ'S HISTORY[3]

Océ is a multinational company providing digital printing systems, software and services for offices, educational institutions, advertising and the graphic design sector. The core of Océ's business is twofold:

- Digital Document Systems: these are copy and print applications for use in offices.
- Wide Format Printing Systems: this business unit is global leader in the area of printing solutions for architects.

Océ has offices in over 30 countries and sells its products in over 90. Until 1997, the company name was Océ van der Grinten. The 'Van der Grinten' part of the name is a reminder of the company's history.

Océ was founded by a chemist, Lodewyk van der Grinten. He owned a dispensing chemist's in the town of Venlo in the Netherlands. There was a surplus of chemist's shops in this city, and a big family was to be maintained. He was therefore continuously on the lookout for new sources of income. Having a great passion for chemical research and developing new preparations, he ended up deploying his skills in the latter area to make some extra money.

In 1877 this resulted in a preparation for colouring margarine. This was the basis for a prospering butter colouring factory, which was eventually sold to Unilever in 1970. But before that, Lodewyk's son had taken the reins of the company in 1890, and with great success. From 1919, his three sons joined the company, which in the 1920s was at the start of the development of techniques that later led to the founding of the present-day photocopier empire. The company name was derived from the revolutionary technique 'Ohne Componenten', which was completed with an additional 'e' at the end to make it pronounceable.

Before World War II, the three Van der Grinten brothers basically only used their business to fund their research into photosensitive materials. They considered themselves researchers first and foremost, followed by inventors, scientists, and only after that businessmen. Océ's strong

continued . . .

pioneering and innovative drive is still the pivot around which the company's value creation evolves. Océ currently holds fifth place on the lists of the Netherlands' main research centres.

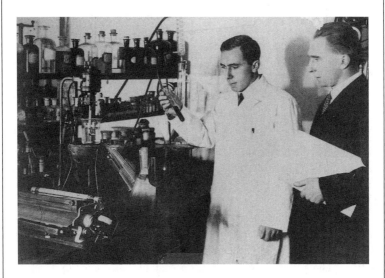

Karel (left) and Louis van der Grinten in the lab (1928).

A company's historical character is firmly embedded in an organization, and greatly influences the orientation, core competencies, vision and mission, as well as the corporate culture and values of the organization. The following section will pick up on the concept of business orientation.

2.3 Business orientation

Business orientation is a concept that refers to the dominant focus within an organization. This focus or orientation can be one of four types: product, process, market or organization focus. Figure 2.3 plots these four orientations in two dimensions: closed versus open, and control versus flexibility. Closed versus open refers to the question of the extent to which an organization is open to external influences. Control versus flexibility refers to the question of how management treats its employees: are employees given a great level of freedom and trust to do their work as well as they can, or are they subjected

	Open	
Control	Market-oriented (they)	Organization-oriented (we)
	Process-oriented (it)	Product-oriented (I)
	Closed	

Flexibility appears to the right; Control to the left.

FIGURE 2.3 Four types of business orientation

to continuous monitoring through different kinds of control mechanisms (such as a time clock)? These four types of orientation can be further denoted using four different pronouns: I, we, they and it.[4] One key step in the positioning process is assessing what type best matches the organization in question.

A *product-oriented* organization bases its marketing efforts on the old adage that we discussed in Chapter 1: 'A good product sells itself.' Product-oriented companies are often good at coming up with and making good-quality products. The company RijkZwaan, for example, succeeded in developing a strain of lettuce (Salanova) with a short stalk, enabling consumers to cut the lettuce leaves from the stalk in one cutting movement (see Box 2.2). Keywords for this kind of organization are quality and innovation. Staff at this kind of company mostly consider professional skills and craftsmanship to be of paramount importance, which goes hand in hand with a high level of education among the workforce. Seeing as the individual – and his or her knowledge and experience in particular – is essential to the organization's realization of a competitive edge, these are often referred to as 'I organizations'. Examples are companies where technology and/or innovations play an important role, such as information and communication technology (ICT) companies, and fresh produce companies, such as RijkZwaan. Such companies often struggle when it comes to extolling the virtues of their brand; product features are often accentuated too much, whereas the benefits they offer customers or emotional purchase motivations are seriously underexposed.

Literature on strategic management refers to product-oriented organizations as 'inside-out companies'. These companies adopt a central focus on manufacturing and creating products. They try to stand out in the market by having unique sources or competencies, such as specific know-how.

BOX 2.2 SALANOVA LETTUCE[5]

'Salanova®. A name that stands for fresh, easy-to-prepare lettuce with big tasting baby-sized leaves. With just one cut the lettuce separates into numerous small, ready-to-eat leaves! Try Salanova yourself and enjoy a delicious fresh salad!

'With this new combination of freshness and convenience you are able to enjoy a totally new quality of lettuce! And this is very interesting, because lettuce is one of the most popular vegetables. And with Salanova that popularity will only increase. Once you have tasted Salanova you will not want any other lettuce. And that is fine, because there is a wide choice of flavours, shapes and colours. So from now on, lettuce has a name: Salanova.'

With some exaggeration, you could say that inside-out companies expect the market to adapt to them. This is reflected in another popular adage: 'Supply creates its own demand.' Inside-out companies often fail to properly monitor their competitors; benchmarking is hardly an issue at these companies. Customers are little more than a 'necessary evil', there to generate revenue.

A *process-oriented* organization places emphasis on the best possible management of its processes (*operational excellence*). This orientation can often be seen in haulage or transport companies, where it comes to the fore in a focus on having the available vehicles run on time. But so-called low-cost companies offering products and services at the lowest possible price also generally focus mainly on their processes. In the optimization of processes it is all about harmonizing all business operations to such an extent that downtime or waste is limited to an absolute minimum. Although every single organization should try to optimize its processes, this does not mean that this orientation always prevails. When something goes wrong at a Toyota plant in Japan, for example, the production line will be shut down if need be, in order to eradicate the problem once and for all. But still, you cannot say Toyota is primarily a process-oriented company.

Process-oriented organizations are also referred to as 'It organizations'. The word 'it' refers to material matters here, such as systems, procedures and premises. Instead of being on people, this type of organization's focus is mainly on things and procedures.

A *market-oriented* organization is driven by the opportunities and chances offered by a market. One typical comment you may hear at such market-driven companies is: 'It's better to have a market than a mill.' Market-oriented companies mostly start out by scouting out the market, mapping customer needs, and then looking into how to produce the desired product. These are so-called 'They organizations'.

Market-oriented organizations sometimes apply an overly blinkered approach to expanding their market expertise, leading them to restrict their operations to marketing products, and having these made elsewhere. A well-known example is Nike. This company has outsourced its production activities to a range of different companies outside the USA. Market-oriented companies are often very good at listening to the customer. This is expressed in the fact that they tend to have great quantities of market research done to stay abreast of what (potential) customers want. A market orientation focuses not only on the customer, but also on the competitor. But some market-driven companies go too far in their market orientation in that they become too preoccupied with (beating) their competitors. When that happens, the customer tends to lose out. In our opinion, a market orientation should never have such a strong competitive focus that it is at the expense of the customer focus.

A fine example of a market-oriented company is Richard Branson's baby Virgin, which he founded in 1970. Virgin currently employs about 50,000 people in 30 countries. It operates in different sectors, ranging from mobile telephony to travel, from financial services to music and from retail to publishing. The way in which Virgin decides to enter a certain market is made explicit under the header 'What we're about' on the Virgin website (see Box 2.3). Looking at Virgin's ventures, you can see that a customer focus dominates in some of them, but that in others they were too eager to beat the competition, leading to the relevance of the brand to consumers not receiving enough attention (as was the case with Virgin Cola).

BOX 2.3 VIRGIN'S MARKET ORIENTATION[6]

'We believe in making a difference. Virgin stands for value for money, quality, innovation, fun and a sense of competitive challenge. We deliver a quality service by empowering our employees and we facilitate and monitor customer feedback to continually improve the customer's experience through innovation.

'When we start a new venture, we base it on hard research and analysis. Typically, we review the industry and put ourselves in the customer's shoes to see what could make it better. We ask fundamental questions: is this an opportunity for restructuring a market and creating competitive advantage? What are the competitors doing? Is the customer confused or badly served? Is this an opportunity for building the Virgin brand? Can we add value? Will it interact with our other businesses? Is there an appropriate trade-off between risk and reward?

'We are also able to draw on talented people from throughout the Group. New ventures are often steered by people seconded from other parts of Virgin, who bring with them the trademark management style, skills and experience. We frequently create partnerships with others to combine industry specific skills, knowledge and operational expertise.'

Literature on strategic management refers to market-oriented organizations as 'outside-in companies'.[7] These are companies that tailor their products to the wishes of the market to the greatest possible degree. Their objective is acquiring a sizeable market share by giving the brand the best possible market position. Concepts such as benchmarking (comparing yourself with top performers in your market) and customer value analysis (calculating or assessing the turnover that will be generated with a customer) are widely used at this kind of company.

An *organization-oriented* organization focuses primarily on motivating its staff and optimizing collaboration between employees. This kind of organization often gives its employees a large degree of freedom (through trust), but equally expects top performance in return. Many organization-oriented organizations do not have a separate brand policy or marketing department; staff members at such organizations are generally marked by a strong customer-driven attitude.

The concept of an 'organization-oriented organization' may seem a rather odd combination of terms. This kind of company intends to build 'internal clockwork' with a differentiating, self-willed culture. But it should be remembered here that an organization-oriented organization is far from being closed to the outside world, despite its unflinching culture. This kind of company is often very alert to customer queries and does not hesitate to take immediate action when faced with negative publicity. Alongside this, such organizations are very keen to strike partnerships with other parties. Starbucks, for example, was at one point accused of not paying a fair price to third-world coffee farmers, and the company responded by setting up the Care programme for these farmers. The openness of this company is also reflected in the partnerships it has struck up with other parties, most notably United Airlines, which serves Starbucks coffee on its planes, and Barnes & Noble, where you can sip a Starbuck Latte while browsing the books. Another American company that can truly be considered an organization-oriented organization is the mother of all budget airlines, Southwest Airlines (see Box 2.4).

The essence of the Southwest Airlines case is that they created an internal community of people who take great pleasure from providing the best possible service to their customers. That is expressed in a quote from its founder:

> We are not an airline with great customer service. We are a great customer service organization that happens to be in the airline business.

It is therefore with good reason that we have branded Southwest Airlines an organization-oriented organization.

BOX 2.4 SOUTHWEST AIRLINES[8]

Right from the day it started flying (1971), Southwest Airlines has been doing things differently from other airlines. A first revolutionary move was to shun major, well-known airports, and instead fly from smaller, easily reachable airports. And Southwest did not choose the usual hub-and-spoke network for its flights either, but instead offered direct connections between cities. These direct flights were not offered twice or four times a day, but often as many as 20 times a day! The latter meant that planes had to be able to land, unload and take off again within a very short time span, in order to stick to the tight schedule. Southwest soon managed to have a plane take off again within 15 minutes of arriving; during busy periods it sometimes happened that the CEO himself would lend a helping hand in the unloading and loading of an airplane. Southwest was the first airline in the USA to introduce phenomenally low prices; in the 1970s you could fly Southwest from San Antonio to Dallas and only have to fork out $13. That pricing strategy is still the same today. European budget airlines EasyJet and Ryanair copied Southwest's proposition.

The former CEO always maintained the goal of building an organization in which everyone feels respected and is given ample opportunity for personal development. In that light, it is no surprise that he even went so far as to say that Southwest employees, and not customers, come first. And you can really tell. Despite currently employing over 32,000 people, the company never loses sight of the personal ups and downs of its staff members. And although employees come first, customer satisfaction ratings are through the roof. The focus on employees has led to great levels of efficiency in all echelons of the organization. Where each Southwest employee serves an average of 2400 customers per year, its closest competitor only manages a number just below 1200 customers per employee per year. Based on results from the period between 1980 and 1999, you can conclude that Southwest Airlines was the best-performing company in the US (with an average ROI of 21.8 per cent), a position it has maintained up to the present day.

In closing

When positioning a brand, it is important to know whether you are dealing with a product-, process-, market-, or organization-oriented company. The business orientation will determine to a large degree what adversity you will encounter when positioning a brand. With some level of exaggeration, you can say that market-oriented companies will not soon receive broad internal support when stressing product features, and that managers at product-oriented companies will not soon appreciate suggestive, immaterial benefits. You should be mindful of the fact that organizations can actually have multiple orientations – companies are rarely purely product-, process-, market- or organization-oriented. A great number of organizations are dominant in one of these four orientations, and have another well-developed orientation on the side. We are therefore dealing with gradations in a continuum.

It is important for any type of organization to define what it is good at and what it struggles with. You are then basically charting the organization's core competencies. In the next section we will outline how core competencies relate to the orientation of an organization.

2.4 Core competencies

On the basis of the history of an organization and an analysis of its business orientation, you can assess where the specific strengths of that organization lie, and what has brought it its greatest victories over its competitors. Strengths can lie in the ability to realize technological breakthroughs (Dyson, for example), in the guarantee that a specific process will always be completed within a certain time span (such as the 'guaranteed overnight delivery' service offered by various logistics service providers), in knowing how to meet a specific customer need (Unilever), or in the art of building an organization where people can develop themselves both in a professional and in a personal sense (such as at Southwest Airlines).

In management literature these examples of specific strengths are referred to as 'core competencies'. Walmart, America's largest retailer, has developed a core competency in the area of stock management. Virgin Airways has honed a service competency based on keen knowledge of customers, an ability to adapt to changing market circumstances and a market-driven approach. Apple has always managed to come up with computers with unrivalled user-friendliness in combination with attractive design. This core competency has served Apple well over the years, especially when it entered the MP3 player market with the launch of the iPod in 2001, the mobile phone market with the iPhone, and recently opening up a whole new product category with the iPad in 2010.

Core competencies cannot be bought like buildings, raw materials and land – they have to develop over time, which is no good for companies in a hurry. An important advantage of this is that competitors cannot easily copy core competencies. A core competency can be the basis of a sustainable competitive advantage (SCA). A core competency can grow into an SCA if it meets the three following prerequisites (see Figure 2.4):

- Grounding: the competency in question has to be firmly grounded in the organization. This means that for a competency to grow into an SCA, it must not be a competency that was purchased or hired.
- Relevance: the competency has to be relevant to customers. For product- and process-oriented organizations in particular, this is something they have to work on, as it is not one of their founding principles. These kinds of companies mostly spend their early years looking for ways of making their differentiating power relevant to customers.
- Differentiation: the competency has to be unique, and not easy to copy by competitors, if it is to yield an SCA. What is striking here is that uniqueness mostly comes about through a differentiating combination of several different core competencies, and not purely on the basis of a single core competency.

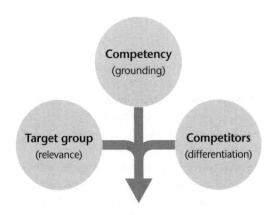

FIGURE 2.4 Relation between core competencies and a sustainable competitive advantage

- SCAs are an important starting point for an organization's strategic brand policy, which includes the positioning of that organization's brands.

Different kinds of core competencies

We can discern a number of different kinds of core competencies. And these can subsequently be categorized in the following four business orientations (see Section 2.3):

- product-oriented: innovation and production;
- process-oriented: internal logistics and external logistics;
- market-oriented: knowledge of the market and customer contact;
- organization-oriented: employee motivation and collaboration.

Innovation

Innovation is a core competency of organizations that stand out for their innovative product development: Hewlett-Packard, for example, with its payoff 'HP. Invent'. Google also possesses ample technological expertise, which manifests itself in the development of new software. The combination of extensive research, development of the perfect search engine and a continuous improvement drive further underline their technological excellence (see Box 2.5).

BOX 2.5 GOOGLE'S TECHNOLOGICAL EXPERTISE[9]

'The perfect search engine', says co-founder Larry Page, 'would understand exactly what you mean and give back exactly what you want. When Google began, you would have been pleasantly surprised to enter a search query and immediately find the right answer. Google became successful precisely because we were better and faster at finding the right answer than other search engines at the time.

'But technology has come a long way since then, and the face of the Web has changed. Recognizing that search is a problem that will never be solved, we continue to push the limits of existing technology to provide a fast, accurate and easy-to-use service that anyone seeking information can access, whether they're at a desk in Boston or on a phone in Bangkok. We've also taken the lessons we've learned from search to tackle even more challenges.'

A special form of innovation is design expertise. This includes not only styling and design, such as used at Apple and Citroën, but also that special talent of spotting trends in that area. And it also involves using this information about trends in the design of new products. Fashion designers, such as Giorgio Armani and Stella McCartney, are a fine example here. And H&M even manages to marry a strong design competency to sharp pricing structures.

Differentiation through an R&D-based core competency is not the exclusive reserve of companies that are all about technology. Banks and insurance companies, for example, can also differentiate their products and services by investing time and money in the development of successful new financial products.

Production

Some organizations have the ability to make something that others can't – for example, a pharmaceutical company that has the capacity to make medicine in superhygienic production facilities. Or Dutch life sciences and materials sciences giant DSM, which has the unique ability to produce a fibre that is 15 times stronger than steel but is also ultralight and even floats on water (brand name Dyneema). In services, this expertise comes to the fore in a company's organizational skills. An example is ID&T, a company that excels at organizing large-scale dance events (see Box 2.6).

Internal logistics

A good example to give you an idea of the competency of internal logistics is provided by supermarkets. Every supermarket chain needs clear internal process expertise to even be a mere player in this sector, let alone a major player. The German supermarket chain Aldi stands out as a result of its low prices and clever purchasing techniques, while the British chain Tesco manages to offer its customers a wide range of fresh products every day. But Toyota also has a strong focus on optimizing internal processes. This does not necessarily have to be about logistics in the sense of shifting goods – it can also be about optimization of the ordering process within an organization.

One special form of internal process expertise is cost leadership. This strategy involves an organization making its processes as cost-efficient as possible, in order to at least not be more expensive than its competitors. A globally operating consultancy firm once worked out how much they would save if all the bins were removed and replaced by one single large bin

34 Corporate identity (Step 1)

> ### BOX 2.6 SENSATION WHITE: AN EVENT FOR 40,000 DANCE FANATICS
>
> ID&T started organizing large-scale dance events in the 1990s. And they are currently conquering the world with their formula 'Sensation: The World's Leading Dance Event'. For these major events to be a success, the company behind them needs a high level of organizational expertise.
>
>

per department. This showed that the cost savings resulting from needing to empty fewer bins were considerable. Internal cost orientation does not necessarily have to be used externally. That is to say, such an orientation does not automatically mean that the corresponding brand will have to be positioned as a budget brand.

External logistics

Some companies have developed competencies in the best possible streamlining of their external logistics. The postal company TNT realized that it was particularly good at transporting letters or parcels from A to B within an agreed time span. Based on this realization, the company went on to sponsor the United Nations World Food Programme: not only by pumping money into the programme, but also by contributing its transport expertise. Courier services, such as DHL, tend to be very frank about using their logistic core competency in their positioning.

Market knowledge

Albert Heijn is the only major grocery store chain in the Netherlands that has marketing off to a tee – not only in terms of taking stock of the wishes and needs of the market (market knowledge), but also in terms of its communication towards customers. Based on its understanding of the customer, Albert Heijn offers more services and a wider assortment of products. Customers are even willing to pay a little more for the added benefits offered by Albert Heijn. The Dutch brewery Grolsch also excels in the area of marketing expertise. Extensive market research is always at the basis of new product versions and categories.

Customer contact

Market knowledge and customer contact are two different things. Market knowledge means that an organization succeeds in charting the customer's wishes. Customer contact, on the other hand, means that an organization succeeds in establishing effective communication with its customers. Some organizations know exactly what their customers want, but subsequently struggle to express that in their communication. UPC's Dutch subsidiary was one company facing this problem: it had market knowledge in abundance, but disastrous communication about its services. This situation persisted until the CEO changed track in 2004/2005. Under the code name 'reconnect', UPC restored contact with customers and even scooped the Golden Contact Centre Award for the best customer service in the Netherlands. Word has it that the CEO posted numerous Post-It notes with all the complaints and reported problems on a wall at UPC head office. Within the time frame he set, all these complaints were handled and resolved one by one.

Employee motivation

One of the hardest core competencies to develop is that of a motivated workforce (an organization-oriented competency). Or, in the words of an

American manager: 'The soft stuff is the hard stuff.' Employee motivation turns out to thrive in a culture typified by flexibility and trust. In 2002, Interpolis, a Dutch insurance company, launched an initiative to win its employees' trust. One of the aspects of this trust-building exercise was the installation of a 'self-scan' cashier system at the company restaurant, so that employees prepared their own bills. In organizations that consider mutual trust to be of paramount importance, employee motivation is considerably higher than at overly rules-driven organizations. Added advantages of a high level of employee motivation are less absence through sickness, low employee turnover and high productivity.

Collaboration

As well as motivating staff, the art of getting people to work together is another aspect of organization-oriented competencies. An organization can only function well if its employees are willing to assist each other in providing the customer with the best possible service. We often see that product- and process-oriented organizations are made up of separate islands or silos, with the different departments basically forming separate, isolated small entities within the organization. Particular skills (i.e. competencies) are required to get departments to work together. There are also cases where employees feel that management distances itself too much from them. Again, you can conclude that if both parties – management and staff – were to develop better collaboration, the operating results would greatly benefit. Just think back to the Southwest Airlines case.

2.5 Vision and mission

An organization's vision and mission follow on from its history, business orientation and core competencies. The literature on the subject does not provide a single, unequivocal explanation of what a vision and a mission exactly are, and what the difference between the two terms is. In this book, we are going by the following definitions:

- A *vision* is a brief and clear-cut forecast of what the market will be like in 5–10 years' time. It mainly focuses on the development of supply and demand in markets that are relevant to the organization. For example, a possible vision formulated by telecommunications and Internet service providers in the mid-1990s could have been that their markets would

amalgamate within 10 years' time (a phenomenon we have come to know as 'triple play', the integration of TV, Internet and telephony). A company's vision is basically its *vision of the future*.
- A *mission* is a catchy description of the way in which the organization intends to realize its objectives within the framework set by the vision. The mission describes the role the organization wants to play in the future as outlined in its vision. A more general term for mission is the self-imposed objective for the coming 5–10 years.

The added value offered by having a vision and a mission lies in:

- Think: do staff members subscribe to the contents of the vision and the mission? In other words, do they agree with it?
- Feel: do the vision and the mission really 'touch' staff members?
- Do: do staff members feel called upon to help realize the vision and the mission? In other words, are they willing to work on it?

In the following we will briefly discuss the concepts of vision and mission. Formulating a *vision* that hits the mark is quite tricky. It requires the skill of someone with many years of experience in a market, as well as the right sensitivity and a profound and wide-ranging knowledge of developments in the area of the products in question, and of the wishes and needs of the target group. But this does not automatically mean a catchy mission will ensue. No matter how accurate and adequate your vision of future market developments is, when a company fails to convert that insight into a powerful mission, the vision will offer little added value to the growth of the company. Various authors in this field are of the opinion that you should aim high when formulating a mission. A mission that merely says 'we want to provide the best quality to achieve maximum customer satisfaction' is hardly inspiring, and will not egg employees on either.

American research has shown that corporate *missions* are much of a muchness.[10] In 300 missions of different major companies, researchers noted 211 mentions of the word 'customers', 206 of the word 'service', 169 of the word 'quality', 158 of the word 'employees', and over 100 of the words 'growth', 'profit', 'respect', 'shareholders' and 'success'. Authors who say that a mission should even be overdone a little are advising that we formulate missions that seem almost unattainable. Such a gutsy mission is also known as a 'Big, Hairy, Audacious Goal' (in short BHAG, pronounced 'bee-hag').[11] Upon taking office as Starbucks CEO, Howard Schultz said he wanted to double the number of franchises from 17 to 34 within a year. A bold statement, considering it had taken Starbucks 17 years to accumulate those 17 franchises. A year later, Schultz had only just failed to deliver on his mission; at the end of 1988, Starbucks had 33 outlets.

Google's mission gets right to the point in the first sentence with the role it wants to play in the future: 'to organize the world's information and make it accessible and useful' (see Box 2.7). Google tries to live up to this claim by maintaining a central focus on the user, i.e. Google's customer. That means keeping search results and advertising strictly separated at all times, and maintaining a continuous improvement drive for its services.

The matrix of Table 2.1 also comes in handy here to further outline the vision and mission of product-, process-, market- and organization-oriented organizations respectively. As we have said, a vision contains a 5- to 10-year market forecast. Product-oriented organizations often possess the know-how

---

BOX 2.7 GOOGLE'S MISSION[12]

'Our mission is to organize the world's information and make it universally accessible and useful. We believe that the most effective, and ultimately the most profitable, way to accomplish our mission is to put the needs of our users first. We have found that offering a high-quality user experience leads to increased traffic and strong word-of-mouth promotion. Our dedication to putting users first is reflected in three key commitments we have made to our users:

- We will do our best to provide the most relevant and useful search results possible, independent of financial incentives. Our search results will be objective and we will not accept payment for inclusion or ranking in them.
- We will do our best to provide the most relevant and useful advertising. Whenever someone pays for something, we will make it clear to our users. Advertisements should not be an annoying interruption.
- We will never stop working to improve our user experience, our search technology, and other important areas of information organization.'

Corporate identity (Step 1) 39

required to make such a forecast (just think back to the 'triple play' example). Most of these types of companies have the ability to adequately define their vision of the market. But they often fail to graduate that into a targeted mission statement, since they have such a strong focus on innovation and providing high-quality products. Product-oriented organizations are often characterized by a powerful vision and a weak mission.

In market-oriented organizations we see the opposite picture to the one painted above for product-oriented organizations. With some degree of exaggeration, you could say that market-oriented organizations are basically clueless regarding future market developments, which leads them to turn to customers to point them in the right direction. They are therefore often lacking a clear vision. But funnily enough, market-oriented organizations do often manage to come up with an accurate and targeted formulation of their objectives. These objectives are mostly formulated in terms of turnover or seizing market share. Market-oriented organizations are often characterized by a weak vision and a powerful mission.

Process-oriented organizations tend to have a weak vision as well as a weak mission. These organizations have insufficient insight into where their market is headed; this is because this kind of organization is less dependent on their external environment (for example (semi-)public bodies). Organization-oriented organizations usually have an accurate idea of what the future may bring for their market (vision). And they also aim high when it comes to formulating a mission. Starbucks CEO Howard Schultz referred to these kinds of mission statements as 'mission statements that have teeth'.

Figure 2.5 summarizes findings relating to visions and missions of product-, process-, market- and organization-oriented organizations.

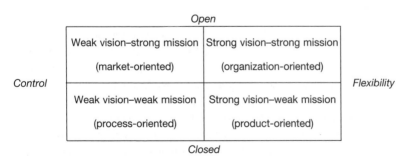

FIGURE 2.5 Strength of a company's vision and mission, linked to business orientation

Visions and mission statements do not necessarily have to be brief and succinct to be inspiring and guiding. Many smaller companies have a 'visionary' leader with a strong 'drive'. The energy of that person often has a more powerful, inspiring and guiding effect than any paper version of visions and mission statements of major companies. Take Marlies Dekkers, for example, a highly successful lingerie designer, who, as far as we know, does not have a formal vision and mission statement. But numerous interviews she has done do paint a clear picture of her vision and mission (see Box 2.8).

BOX 2.8 VISION AND MISSION OF FASHION DESIGNER MARLIES DEKKERS[13]

marlies|dekkers

Vision

'Looking at the timeline of humanity, only a tiny piece of it represents the time in which women have their own money, the pill or are actively participating. We haven't had long to think about what our fantasies are, our desires, what do we enjoy? What it's basically about is seeing things from the point of view of the woman. When 500 years from now, an archaeologist finds my lingerie, he will have to be able to tell that it comes from a time when women were truly free.'

Mission

'Making big bums look smaller, that's something I'm good at. Many women are not happy with their bodies. They look at themselves in the mirror and see the odd flabby mass, and that they are no longer a size 12. Giving those women something back, something they have lost, that is my buzz. In about ten years' time, I want to be a major player in the global lingerie market. It irritates me that in so many countries around the world you can only buy unimaginative and uncomfortable bras. A kind of mission, yes. I want to make as many women as possible feel that there is another way.'

In closing

Up to this point in the chapter we have analysed the identity of an organization on the basis of its history, dominant business orientation, core competencies and the extent to which its vision and mission statement have been developed. We have highlighted that business orientation, core competencies, and vision and mission are subjects that are part of the area of strategic management, and should therefore be substantiated by the management of an organization. When positioning a brand, it is essential that these aspects of strategic management be mapped out, as they set the framework within which the brand can be positioned. Other aspects of corporate identity that define the positioning framework are corporate culture (see Section 2.6) and the values that an organization aims to uphold (Section 2.7).

2.6 Culture

Box 2.1 in Section 2.2 provided a brief outline of the history of Océ. We drew particular attention to this organization's strong innovation-driven operations. This kind of organization often has a different internal culture than companies that operate in a more market-driven manner. Corporate culture relates to matters such as what interpersonal contacts are like within the company, how people address each other, what they consider important, and whether people feel committed to the organization. A company's culture becomes apparent in the behaviour of its staff, the way they dress (formal or informal) and the hierarchy at the organization (is it a 'flat organization' with little distance between management and staff, or a highly hierarchical organization?).

Hofstede defined culture as the way of life or 'mental programming' of a group of people from the same social environment.[14] Culture determines, to a large extent, how an individual thinks, senses and acts. Cultural differences exist between continents (North America versus Europe), countries (France versus Germany), regions (city versus countryside) and professions ('IT people differ greatly from marketing people'), but also between companies (British Airways versus Virgin Atlantic). In the case of organizations, we therefore speak of corporate culture, internal culture or working culture. Corporate culture comes to the fore in expressions such as 'In this organization people don't mind getting their hands dirty.'

From the 1980s, interest in corporate culture has seen a significant increase, leading to greater insight into the influence that corporate culture has on the operating results of organizations. As a general statement, you could say that, before 1980, organizations accentuated management, control and stability. But the focus has shifted to self-management (by employees), flexibility and responsiveness (responding to and adapting to surroundings). Research has shown that changes within organizations are doomed to fail if corporate culture does not change alongside.

Positioning requires great familiarity with the corporate culture. To illustrate this, consider the following situation. Companies' advertising campaigns sometimes revolve around their own staff: for example, an employee showing how far he or she is willing to go to serve a customer. If the picture painted in the advertising campaign does not tally with reality, the chances are that employees will turn their backs on this form of communication. It can lead to them adopting the opposite behaviour. By taking corporate culture into account in the brand positioning process and the final choice of a positioning, you can bypass these kinds of problems. In the following we will therefore further define four different types of corporate culture.

Mapping corporate culture

In order to get a big picture view of the corporate culture of an organization, we use the 'competitive value model'[15] developed by Cameron and Quinn. In line with the four types of business orientation from Figure 2.3, this model distinguishes four different forms of corporate culture: family culture, formal culture, performance culture and adhocracy (see Figure 2.6). In the following sections we will go further into these forms of corporate culture. We will do so by employing a certain level of stereotyping, in order to clearly bring the differences between corporate cultures to the fore.

A *family culture* is generally found in organizations that are product-driven. The concept of family culture refers to the fact that employees feel

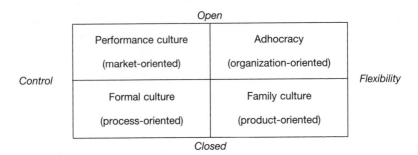

FIGURE 2.6 Four different types of corporate culture

part of one big family. These types of companies are often (originally) family-run businesses. An organization with a family culture aims to create and uphold good internal relations, employee care and (individual) flexibility. But a side effect of such a setup is that individuals are hardly ever held accountable for errors; slip-ups are often glossed over because people shy away from confrontation. Employee loyalty, on the other hand, is relatively high. Employees generally have a job for life at organizations like these. Staff turnover is very low here; 20 or 30 years of service are no exception. In organizations with a family culture, leaders are often mentors (or even father figures) to their staff members. The downside of this type of working culture is that engagements are not always kept, and that the organization is made up of so-called 'islands' or 'silos' – departments that operate more or less autonomously, without effective collaboration between them.

An organization with a *formal culture* is managed rigidly. Employees' internal and external behaviour is regulated by formal processes. Relations between employees are defined by the terms superior and inferior (subordinate). You could also refer to this corporate culture as a 'functional hierarchy', with people placed in fixed roles that are firmly laid down in job descriptions, and with people making a promotion – or getting a raise – if they meet certain functional requirements (such as through a system of periodic salary increments). Most processes in the organization are standardized or regulated. Important characteristics are structure, procedures, formal rules, efficiency, reliable delivery and cost containment. Leaders act as coordinators and organizers. There are also downsides to this type of working culture, namely the fact that employees are not encouraged to bring up improvement points, and are hardly stimulated to adopt a customer-driven attitude in their thinking and actions. With some exaggeration, you can say that employees at these kinds of organizations are after security, i.e. they work to live.

A *performance culture* is generally found at organizations that are market-driven. This kind of organization has, just like an organization with a formal culture, a hierarchical setup. But in this setup employees are held accountable for their performance, and not so much on the basis of the functional requirements of their jobs. Organizations with a performance culture have a strong competitive drive, not only towards competitors, but also internally. As we pointed out earlier, market-oriented companies keep close tabs on the competition, and have a strong drive to outperform competitors. Internally these kinds of companies are also marked by ruthless competition, which is reflected in the 'up' or 'out' principle in their promotions policy (you either move up or move out; there is no room for stagnation). Employees at these companies are explicitly held responsible for their performance and behaviour. This is a culture that makes great demands on people; aggressiveness and a strong will to win are basic characteristics of a performance-driven corporate culture. Leaders assume a no-nonsense approach to management, and errors often lead to the rolling of heads. The problem with a performance culture is that it can backfire. Companies with such a strong performance-based culture often have high levels of absenteeism and a certain degree of passivity (lethargy). In a performance culture employees will be less likely to take the initiative to correct flaws in the organization.

An organization with an *adhocracy*[16] is highly dynamic and flexible, its orientation is generally on organizational excellence. In an adhocracy work is mainly done on a project basis, with decisions made with an eye to optimizing the execution conditions for the project (not obstructed by any bureaucratic rules). An adhocratic organization is therefore highly flexible and dynamic, and has a true entrepreneurial spirit. Individual interests play second fiddle to group interests; the emphasis is on teamwork, consensus and participation. Seeing as individual interests never or hardly ever prevail, staff motivation levels are often through the roof. This translates into low levels of absenteeism, low staff turnover and exceptionally high levels of dedication in staff. Employees are, in other words, extremely committed to the company. This kind of organization is often seen as 'different' – something people at the organization itself often take great pride in (such as at Southwest Airlines and Google). We have already drawn attention to the fact that organization-oriented organizations attach great importance to innovations and 'mental market leadership' (wanting to take the lead in the market). Leaders in this kind of organization are characterized by an entrepreneurial spirit, an innovatory attitude and a willingness to take risks. The downside is that an employee will have to adapt to the organization if he wants to keep his job. The distinct culture at adhocratic organizations often leaves little room for employees who are unwilling to conform to this culture.

Although all these different cultural profiles will apply to an organization to varying degrees, every organization will, in principle, have one dominant corporate culture type. Unilever, for example, has a performance culture with a strong focus on its external image and the turnover generated by the individual product brands. Most state services are characterized by a formal culture where controlled processing of information is key. Employees at KLM Airlines (part of Air France-KLM) are highly loyal towards their employer and call themselves 'blue' after the dominating colour in the KLM logo and housestyle. This indicates a strong family culture at KLM. Google stimulates individuality and entrepreneurship, with employees working in project teams without a fixed hierarchy, which is a common feature in an adhocracy. Some companies have in the past succeeded in effecting a necessary and drastic corporate culture change. An example is Océ (see Box 2.9).

BOX 2.9 CORPORATE CULTURE CHANGE AT OCÉ[17]

Up to the 1950s, Océ van der Grinten was a family-run business. The three brothers at the company's helm aimed to provide lasting financial security for their employees and their families. Océ was all about innovation, in combination with responding to market developments and opportunities offered by the market. The brothers personally regulated all processes to the very last detail. These were years of boisterous growth, with developments in the Central European market requiring expansion of operations, as well as investment, formalization, delegation of responsibility and risk-taking.

Records from that period show that the brothers did realize that they themselves lacked the ability to further expand the business and lead it into the next stage. To their credit, the brothers chose to bring in a director from outside the family. The choice for the new CEO was typical. As a psychologist, he fitted right in with the way the family ran the company, setting great store by companionship, team spirit and social commitment. And in his role of director of a psychological agency, the new CEO had a track record of realizing growth. In the period after this appointment, Océ was converted from a small solid company into a multinational. Non-technical staff was brought in from outside the organization (starting with a legal counsel and a marketing professional). And Océ was floated on the stock market, which brought in outside capital for takeovers and the setup of its own sales organization.

The internal climate at the Océ organization changed gradually. The management charted a clear course, and delegated responsibilities for the attaining of objectives. What ensued was a period of tempestuous growth, followed by consolidation. Turnover and profits were multiplied. Turnover grew from €7m in 1957 to just under €60m in 1967.

Corporate culture and positioning

Corporate culture is an increasingly important element in the positioning process. On the one hand, we are seeing the service-providing aspect of operations gain in importance. In our modern service and information-based society, providing a good service is the best way to create added value. That makes contact between employees and customers the determining factor in the building of a brand image. The nature of this contact is shaped by the way in which an employee thinks, feels and acts, as inspired by the corporate culture. On the other hand, there is the greater visibility of the corporate brand behind the product (the organization explosion), which we outlined in Chapter 1. A corporate brand is charged by the attitude and behaviour of the members of that organization to a greater degree than a product brand is. Finally, there is ever more scientific proof to back up the claim that changes in organizations are bound to be unsuccessful if the corporate culture does not change as well. The same goes for positionings that require an attitude and behaviour change in employees.

Successful organizations stand out for their unique culture that provides security, clarity and continuity, and creates a common identity and sense of direction. The common identity of an organization is expressed through tried-and-tested corporate and customer values, which is the final pending aspect of corporate identity.

2.7 Corporate and customer values

Values refer to ideals that people pursue. Honesty, transparency, trust and care are examples of such values. Not only do we find it important to pursue such values, but the very pursuance of such values in itself can give us a positive boost. Most people will, for example, prefer to work at a company that pursues values that dovetail with their own, instead of at one where these values are not the guiding principle for the thinking and actions of that company. Values are emotionally charged, and determine to a considerable degree whether employees feel committed to the organization or not.

When discussing values, you can split them up into corporate values, customer values and brand values. *Corporate values* are those values (and standards) that the organization as a whole considers important, such as corporate social responsibility, sustainability, stimulating entrepreneurship in the organization, being a good employer and corporate governance. These values can be aimed at employees, investors, suppliers, media, special interest groups, the government and the general public. *Customer values* are basically a specific form of corporate values, i.e. values that an organization considers important in its dealings with its customers, such as simplicity, sustainability and security. Customer values should follow on from corporate values; they should in any case never contradict the values of the organization in question. Both corporate and customer values are aspects of the corporate identity. Customer values are aimed at external customers, and reflect the organization's philosophy on how to deal with (the interests of) its customers. When defining *brand values*, you are, in fact, deciding which corporate and customer values you intend to use to present the brand. After all, brand positioning

Corporate identity (Step 1) **47**

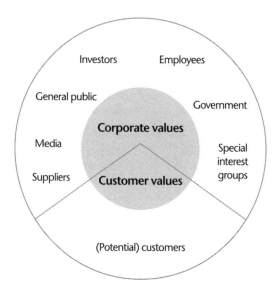

FIGURE 2.7 Different target groups for corporate and customer values

requires an organization to choose which aspects of its identity it wants to present to the outside world in order to raise its profile. In terms of values, this means that the organization also has to decide which corporate and customer values it wants to stress. How to define brand values is further explained in Chapter 6 (Step 5: positioning). In this present section we will now further go into corporate and customer values. Figure 2.7 summarizes the relevant target groups for corporate and customer values.

Both corporate and customer values are defined within the organization. But external factors can also lead to certain values. Alarming pollution levels, for example, and the pressure that different groups are exerting on companies to make their production more sustainable, have led to a range of organizations stressing sustainability as part of their values set. This sort of influence also affects customer values. In 2008 fierce criticism was directed at many banking agencies about extensive bonuses. Expectations are that these companies will modify not only their conduct towards their customers, but also their customer values, for example by emphasizing 'transparency'. Table 2.1 summarizes a number of common corporate values, and provides examples of customer values. We have arranged these values per target group, and by splitting them up into the 'what versus how' dimension.

In practice, corporate values often turn out to be far from unique. About 90 per cent of all organizations claim corporate values from among those

TABLE 2.1 Examples of corporate values and customer values

		Corporate values		Customer values
Who	Employees	Investors	Government/ media/special interest groups/ suppliers/ general public	(Potential) customers
What	Quality Service Innovation Success	Value Growth Profit	Environmental awareness Sustainable Social contribution	Simplicity Health Sustainability
How	Customer- driven Respectful Result- driven Enterprising	Reliable Aggressive	Responsible Ethical Committed Transparent	Convenience Closeness Security

listed in Table 2.1.[18] That undermines the differentiating effect of corporate values, and makes them implausible. Real and valuable differentiation is only achieved by the way values are implemented. TNT, for example, decided not to renew its sponsorship deal with the Dutch Open golf tournament in 2002. In order to back up the corporate value 'social commitment', the chairman of the TNT board opted to use sponsorship funds for the UN World Food Programme, which would also benefit from TNT's expertise in logistics. Partly due to the fact that this kind of move was unprecedented, it meant a serious boost to TNT's reputation and their employees' pride, and saw TNT climb up the rankings of most attractive employers.

In closing

In this chapter we have described six factors of corporate identity. Where strategic management is concerned, we have distinguished four types of organ-izations (product-, process-, market- and organization-oriented). Table 2.2 lists the main findings regarding business orientation, core competencies, vision, mission and culture. In the following chapter we will discuss the brand architecture of a company at length.

TABLE 2.2 Summary of four of the six factors of corporate identity

Open

	Market-oriented:	Organization-oriented:
	• They-oriented • Core competencies: market knowledge, customer contact • Weak vision–strong mission • Performance culture	• We-oriented • Core competencies: employee motivation, collaboration • Strong vision–strong mission • Adhocracy
	Process-oriented:	Product-oriented:
	• It-oriented • Core competencies: internal and external logistics • Weak vision–weak mission • Formal culture	• I-oriented • Core competencies: innovation, production • Strong vision–weak mission • Family culture

Control ——————————————————————— *Flexibility*

Closed

Notes

1. We have already pointed out in Chapter 1 that we will not be using the term 'product' to purely denote a physical (tangible) object, but also to include services.
2. Kapferer (2008, pp. 28–29).
3. Van der Velden (2007).
4. After: Coppenhagen (2002).
5. Source: www.salanova.net (accessed 30 December 2010).
6. Source: www.virgin.com (accessed 30 December 2010).
7. See de Wit and Meyer (2005) on the paradox of markets and resources.
8. Sources: Southwest Airlines Site; Cameron and Quinn (2006, pp. 3–4, 97); Freiberg and Freiberg (1997).
9. Source: www.google.com/corporate (accessed 16 December 2010).
10. Abrahams (1999).
11. Collins and Porras (1997).
12. Source: Google Prospectus.
13. Sources: *Telegraaf* newspaper (9 August 2002) and *NRC Handelsblad* newspaper (10 July 2003).
14. Hofstede and Hofstede (2007).
15. Cameron and Quinn (2006).

16 The term 'adhocracy' is a contraction of the Latin words *ad hoc* (for a specific case) and the suffix '-cracy' (as in 'democracy'), which comes from the Greek word *kratein* ('have the power', 'rule'). Adhocracy literally means that decisions are made on the basis of arguments that are relevant to the matter at hand, and not on the basis of general organization-wide arguments and rules (such as in a bureaucracy).
17 Van der Velden (2007).
18 Abrahams (1999); Van Lee *et al.* (2005).

3
BRAND ARCHITECTURE (STEP 2)

In the previous chapter we presented a model that you can use to map the corporate identity of your organization. Alongside this information about corporate identity, you will also have to take the organization's other brands into account. When an organization has two brands in the same market, for example, the positioning of one brand has to be geared to the positioning of the other. Tackling these issues comes under the realm of *brand architecture*, which, together with corporate identity, makes up the internal analysis within a positioning process. Figure 3.1 presents brand architecture in the BTC model as an additional outer layer around the brand that is being positioned.

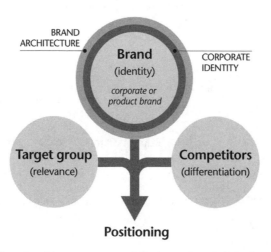

FIGURE 3.1 Brand architecture as part of the internal analysis in the positioning process

Brand architecture is made up of three branches, which we will introduce in Section 3.1. Sections 3.2–3.4 will subsequently discuss these in greater detail. Section 3.5 concludes this chapter with a number of general conclusions on brand architecture.

3.1 The three branches of brand architecture

Brand architecture can be broken up into three branches that can best be described in the following terms:

- Brand-name strategy: does an organization's brand name policy entail the use of its corporate brand or will it enter the market with product brands?
- Brand portfolio: in the case where an organization has chosen to launch several product brands, how will these be geared to each other? A brand portfolio covers the collection of brands in a specific product category a specific provider markets.
- Sub-branding: will sub-brands be used below certain product brands? One example is Vital, a sub-brand of Nivea (Nivea Vital).

Figure 3.2 depicts the three branches of brand architecture in a diagram. Brand-name strategy relates to the question whether a company opts to choose its corporate name as the brand name or uses a specific brand name (names) for its product(s). Brand portfolio management relates to ensuring the different product brands do not clash in the market. Sub-branding refers to the harmonization of product brands and sub-brands.

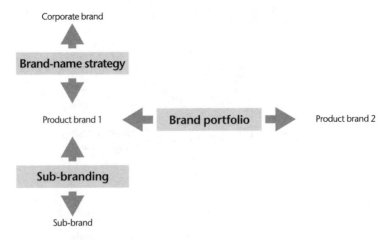

FIGURE 3.2 Diagram of the three branches of brand architecture

3.2 Brand-name strategy

An organization can choose to deploy its own name as the brand name, or to market one or several specific product brand names. When using its corporate name as the brand name, this name will generally be derived from the trading name as recorded in the trade register. For example, electronics giant Philips' entry in the trade register is in full 'Royal Philips Electronics NV'. But when we make reference to the name of the corporate brand, we are referring to the name as used in the market (i.e. Philips). An organization that chooses to only market its product(s) under the corporate brand is in fact using one single brand name. Complex organizations – mostly those formed after (successive) mergers – may have several corporate brands to choose from. In order not to complicate matters too much, in this chapter we will assume that an organization has one corporate brand name only.

A positioning process throws up two brand name strategic questions:

1   Does an organization use the corporate brand name in the market, or does it use specific product brand names?
2   If an organization uses product brands, does it do so alongside the name of its corporate brand? Take Nestlé, for example, which uses several product brands, but many of these products also mention the corporate brand Nestlé. This question is the so-called 'endorsement question'. Remember that products can be either goods or services; this makes new luxury airline OpenSkies a product brand endorsed by corporate brand British Airways. OpenSkies was initially even called 'OpenSkies by BA', with the word 'by' being the ultimate endorsement indicator, as also used by Levi Strauss to push its cheaper brand Signature (Signature by Levi Strauss).

The choices an organization makes in answering both these questions have implications for the brand that is being positioned.

Corporate brand or product brand?

Setting up an organization involves choosing a name under which that organization will be operating. An organization will therefore always have a corporate name. Most organizations soon face the question of whether their products should have their own names or not. There are various conceivable reasons why an organization should use product brands. The most obvious one is that product brands make it easier to tailor supply to the wishes and needs of different target groups. You can then launch different product brands, each targeting different target groups and different wishes and needs. This is rather trickier for an organization that uses only its corporate brand, even more so when considering that a brand has to stand for one clearly demarcated proposition (promise). The audiovisual design brand Bang & Olufsen, with its exclusive proposition, will always struggle to launch products for a target group that is only moved by low prices. In other words, an organization can better tailor its product to the market using product brands than it can with one corporate brand. Another reason for using product brands is prevention of *image spillover*. Research indicates that more negative image spillover between products occurs when only one brand name is used instead of several visually unrelated brand names.[1]

There are also reasons to favour working with the corporate brand instead of product brands. The first one relates to the convenience and clarity this offers financial investors. When a corporate brand is actively used in approaching financial investors, these could encounter problems if the organization were also to use product brands. The organization, in turn, could meet investors halfway by using the corporate name as an *endorser* on product brands. A second, but certainly not less important, criterion is controlling organizational complexity within the company. Working with one name only (i.e. the corporate brand name) creates maximum clarity internally, hence maximizing the chance of the company succeeding in communicating an unequivocal message. The use of several different product brands alongside a corporate brand could lead to confusion internally, making it harder for people to keep up with which message is to be linked to which brand. A third reason is the increasing pressure from governments, investors and customers for organizations to provide transparency. Openness towards society is easier to provide when an organization has one uniform picture to present, and when this is done in a coordinated fashion.

One final consideration in light of the question whether an organization should only use its corporate brand or go for product brands is that internal feelings sometimes have a greater influence on the answering of this question than what the customer thinks. Again, as an example, we will take Philips, which decided to ditch the dedicated brand name Philishave for its shavers, and replace it by the corporate brand Philips. This decision was not made overnight: five years of internal discussions went into it, mainly revolving around the fact that the Philishave division had always been an (internal) showpiece at Philips. Consumers, however, were much less bothered by this name change.

Asia versus Europe and the USA

The choice to use the corporate brand in the market is also driven by cultural traditions. Many Asian companies use this strategy. One possible explanation for this is that Asian companies depended greatly on political leaders in the 19th and 20th centuries. Families that had been granted a licence to operate by the government often went on to build huge empires producing all sorts of products. Japanese examples of such conglomerates are Hitachi, Sony, Toyota and Yamaha. Yamaha is a company that uses its corporate name for engines, audiovisual equipment and pianos alike. South Korea is another market where companies generally put their corporate brand on all kinds of products, with the best known being LG and Samsung. However, Asian companies have, over time, come to realize that they often struggle to sell different products with a single brand name.[2] That is why they have started to differentiate by introducing product brands to accompany the corporate brand (Yamaha WaveRunner for water scooters) and/or introduce sub-brands (Yamaha WaveRunner FX Cruiser). Sony also uses product brands and/or sub-brands, such as Aibo, Bravia, Camcorder, Cyber-shot, PlayStation, Vaio and Walkman.

In Europe and the USA, we see both types of companies: those that mainly use their corporate brand as the message carrier (for example, McDonald's and Nike) and those that focus mostly on product brands (for example, the Bolton Group, Reckitt Benckiser, General Motors, Unilever and the Volkswagen Group). The latter companies tend to limit the use of their corporate name to a small mention on the back of the packaging or in the small print of the instructions for use (a legal sender). Classical examples are companies such as Procter & Gamble, which markets product brands such as Always, Fairy, Head & Shoulders and Pringles, and Unilever, with Timotei, Flora, Dove and Axe (which goes by the name Lynx in the UK). These giant conglomerates do not use their corporate brand on the front of their product packaging. Unilever, however, is now also using its corporate name in product advertising.

Corporate endorsement

The second question addressed in this section is whether an organization that has opted to use product brands should also give some exposure to its corporate brand. This concerns the use of 'corporate endorsement', i.e. visible use of the name of the corporate brand alongside the name of the product brand.

56 Brand architecture (Step 2)

There are three possible reasons why a company would use its corporate brand name alongside different product brand names. The first is that a corporate brand can back up a product brand in communication to customers. This applies in particular when the corporate brand has greater added value than the product brand. A second reason for making a corporate brand prominent on product packaging is that it enables the company to show (potential) investors what brands the company holds. That may well be the reason why Nestlé puts its name on so many of its products, if not all. A look around the shelves of any French supermarket will make it clear very quickly that Nestlé is a major player. A third reason is closely tied to a company's intention to make sure their own staff knows which brands make up the company's brand portfolio. In May 2004, Unilever launched its new organization logo and announced that it would be placed on all its packaging (see Box 3.1). The CEO of Unilever at that time pointed out that this was intended to make Unilever employees better aware of the group's portfolio of product brands. The real objective of this move was to reinforce the internal culture at Unilever.

BOX 3.1 UNILEVER'S VITALITY MISSION

With a view to preparing itself for the future, Unilever came up with a new mission statement in 2004: 'Vitality is at the heart of Unilever. Our mission is to meet everyday needs for nutrition, home hygiene, and personal care with brands that help people feel good, look good, and get more out of life.' This mission statement highlights people's vitality, and is therefore often referred to as the 'vitality mission'. At the same time, Unilever introduced its new corporate logo to support this mission. This logo is made up of 25 symbols, each of which represents a different aspect of the company:

Sun: our most important natural source of energy; the start of life, the ultimate symbol of vitality. The sun stands for Port Sunlight, the home of the Lever Brothers, as well as of a number of Unilever's brands. The Unilever brands Becel and Omo use sunrays in their logos to bring their strengths to the fore.

continued . . .

DNA: the double helix, the genetic blueprint of all life, and symbol of biosciences; the key to healthy living. Where the sun is the largest building block of life, DNA is the smallest.

Bee: represents creation, pollination, hard work and biodiversity; bees symbolize both challenges and opportunities in environmental issues.

Hand: symbol of sensitivity, care and need; stands for both skin and touch.

Flower: represents smell; in combination with the hand, the flower stands for moisturizing personal care products and lotions.

Hair: symbol of beauty and looking good; combined with the flower, hair represents personal hygiene and scent; combined with the hand, it represents softness.

Palm tree: a cherished resource. Gives us not only palm oil, but also different sorts of fruit, such as coconuts, bananas and dates. Also symbolizes paradise.

Sauces or spreads: stand for mixing and stirring; and also makes reference to flavouring.

Spoon: symbol of nutrition, tasting and cooking.

Bowl: a bowl filled with deliciously aromatic food. Can also stand for a ready-made meal, hot beverage or soup.

Herbs and spices: stand for seasonings and fresh ingredients.

Fish: represents food, sea and fresh water.

Glitter: clean, healthy and brimming with energy.

Bird: symbol of freedom; stands for relaxing after a hard day's work, and for getting more out of life.

Recycling: part of Unilever's efforts in the area of sustainability.

Lips: stands for beauty, looking good and good taste.

Ice cream: a treat, fun and enjoyment.

Tea: a plant or plant extract, such as tea; also a symbol of growth and agriculture.

Particles: refer to science, 'fizzing air bubbles'.

Deepfreeze: the plant symbolizes freshness, the snowflake freezing.

Wave: symbolizes purity, freshness and energy, both for personal care and, in combination with clothes, washing.

Droplets: refer to clean water and purity.

Small jar: stands for packaging – a small jar of body or face cream linked to personal care.

Clothes: stand for fresh washing and looking good.

Heart: symbol of love, care and health.

Brand-name strategy and positioning

The final question to address in this section is what impact a brand name strategy will have on the positioning of the brand in question. If an organization uses only its corporate brand, it will be hard to choose a positioning that is spot-on. Many banks face this problem. If a bank serves both private and business customers, and also sells insurance policies and investment and/or real estate services, such a bank can only choose a rather abstract positioning. This poses a problem not only because the bank then has to water down the positioning of certain products, but also because certain target groups cannot be targeted as keenly as the company would perhaps like. This, in turn, leads to the risk of a corporate brand being perceived as too abstract and nondescript by many people. An advantage of using a corporate brand is that it can inspire immediate confidence in the product carrying the brand name (providing the brand is a well-known one and a relatively major player).[3]

If an organization chooses to use product brands, it will be better able to specifically tailor to certain wishes and needs. And it can also clearly aim its product at certain target groups. The downside is that if it concerns a little-known brand, consumers can be hesitant to buy the product, because they do not fully trust the brand ('unknown, unloved'). This shortcoming can, however, be overcome by using the corporate brand as an endorser to back up the product brand. This means that if the corporate name is used alongside a product brand, both brands can claim their own proposition (making their positioning more targeted). The product brand will then have to clearly commit to a concrete need it is targeting, with the corporate brand claiming associations that go with socially responsible operations of the company. Rockwool, for example, positions its product brands (such as Taurox) in a reasonably instrumental manner by emphasizing product benefits. The corporate brand, on the other hand, is used to provide some emotional charging, because Rockwool is well aware of the fact that both rational and emotional arguments play a role in decision-making. Associations triggered by a corporate brand can relate to the company's corporate social responsibility, the company's expertise in the product class(es) in question and/or emotional reasons for purchase (the latter mainly if motivations for purchase of product features are mainly of a rational or functional nature, as in the case of Taurox and Rockwool). Another good example is Shell, which launched a corporate campaign in 2010 to position the organization as one that, in its own words, 'helps to meet global energy demand in a responsible way'. Alongside this corporate campaign, Shell positions its product brand V-Power with the more functional claim of delivering maximum engine performance.

3.3 Brand portfolio

Leaving the corporate brand for what it is, this section will focus on the use of product brands. The central question in this section is whether you should enter the market with one or several product brands, and what consequences this has for positioning. Research has shown that many companies' brand portfolios are the result of mergers and acquisitions.[4] In other words, brand portfolios are mostly historically determined, and rarely rationally and systematically designed brand collections. In the late 1990s a string of companies decided to rationalize their brand portfolios, mainly due to the fact that often 20 per cent of the brands in a portfolio were yielding 80 per cent of the turnover, and the cost involved in building strong brands had skyrocketed as a result of media fragmentation (see the media explosion described in Section 1.1).

In this section we will first address the question of which criteria are available for the building of a balanced brand portfolio. We will subsequently focus on the rising importance of the price dimension in brand portfolios. And we will wrap this section up with an outline of the consequences of brand portfolio issues on positioning.

Criteria

Three criteria are relevant for the building of a balanced brand portfolio. In order not to overly complicate the decision-making process, we will discuss these criteria in the following order:

1. Contents: do products differ in such a way that they should not come under one and the same brand?
2. Financial: is the financial exploitation basis of a product combination substantial enough to exploit it as a separate brand?
3. Strategic: do future market developments and expected competitor behaviour necessitate an investment in several brands?

We will illustrate the decision-making process surrounding the question whether to opt for one or several product brands using a real-life case set in the Dutch market for yoghurt, yoghurt drinks and desserts. The above criteria were used in the decision-making process that led to the management of a Dutch dairy producer to position a new brand – Vifit – as a separate brand alongside one of its older brands, Mona (see Box 3.2).

Whenever one brand has products with clear proposition differences, the question arises whether some of these products should be carved out of the

BOX 3.2 HOW VIFIT WAS CARVED OUT OF THE MONA BRAND

In 1998 the brand Vifit became the centre of a stormy marketing discussion in the Dutch dairy market. At the time, the brand name Mona adorned two types of products: desserts and yoghurt drinks with a healthy-living claim. The desserts appealed to people's urge for indulgence, which was expressed in the pay-off 'Mona. Dairy Indulgence'. In the preceding four years, Mona had branched out by launching three sub-brands that sought to get a piece of the booming healthy eating action:

- Mona Vifit (1994), with the claim on its packaging that it 'purifies the body and boosts resistance';
- Mona Fysiq (1996): 'helps maintain responsible cholesterol levels';
- Mona Optimel (1998): 'no added sugar, 0 per cent fat, rich in vitamin B, C, and calcium'.

The propositions of these sub-brands seriously clashed with the proposition of the desserts. Where the desserts division pushed a positive motivation for purchase ('all you can eat'), the three sub-brands accentuated a slightly negative motivation for purchase (boosting resistance,

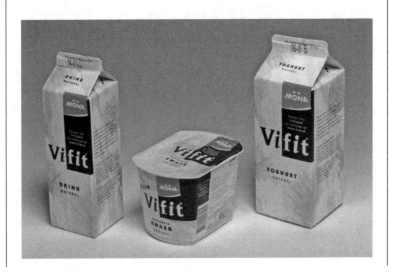

continued . . .

> keeping cholesterol in check and non-fattening). Research showed that the Mona brand was failing to adequately claim the association 'delicious' for its desserts, and equally unsuccessful in having people subscribe to the proposition of the three sub-brands. The Mona brand was basically stuck in the middle, simply because there was too big a gap between the propositions of the desserts on one side and the Vifit, Fysiq and Optimel products on the other.

brand (a so-called 'carve-out operation'). The criterion for deciding whether to carry several brands or only the one involves getting to the bottom of the following two matters:

1. Are there differences in the propositions of products with the same brand name?
2. How much distance is there between the two products? Research has shown that proposition differences only devalue a brand when consumers observe only a small product distance.[5]

Examples of proposition differences

There are a number of conceivable situations where it would be clear beforehand that products do not go well together in a perceptual sense:

- Differences in perceived corporate ability:[6] customers often consider (mostly subconsciously) certain corporate abilities to be compatible or incompatible. For example, is it credible for Philips, which is generally known for making light bulbs, to also manufacture highly complex products, such as computer chips? (It should be noted that Philips has therefore made a conscious choice and effort to get rid of its image as a 'light bulb manufacturer'.)
- Different purchase motivations between products (negative versus positive motivations).[7] An insurance company that focuses on selling personal pension plans with a positive motivation (the good life after working) will have difficulty selling indemnity insurances, which are negatively motivated.
- Highly divergent price propositions: brands that do not target one coherent pricing proposition cannot develop a strong brand. C&A,

for example, used to sell exclusive designer clothes alongside its relatively cheap own-brand clothes (a strategy that obviously did not work). In order to maintain the required coherent pricing proposition, Renault even went so far as to launch cheaper cars under a different name, Dacia.
- Different sensitivities to commerciality. A certification institution issues certificates to companies and products. If such an institution were to be asked to give companies advice beforehand, advice on what they would have to do to merit the certificate, the independence of this institution could be in danger. Seeing as the issuing of certificates is a non-commercial activity – and providing consultancy services is not – both activities do not fit under the same brand.
- Differences between target groups: a brand that is clearly aimed at a young target group will struggle to also appeal to an older target group. Nivea's only option was to create a sub-brand for its anti-aging cream (Nivea Vital).

Distance between products: close or far apart?

Some brands are relatively broad, and others relatively narrow. A broad brand is a brand that graces many different products (such as Virgin). A narrow brand is a brand under which only a limited number of products are marketed (such as Pringles). The question whether to carve products with a different proposition out of your brand depends not only on the proposition difference, but also on the distance to the core product of the brand. We can explain this further using the example of the brand Harley-Davidson (see Box 3.3). Products with a different proposition that are marketed in the same product class as the flagship product can undermine the brand image of the flagship product. For example, if Harley-Davidson were to introduce Harley-Davidson scooters, with TV ads with well-dressed Italian dandies riding around Rome on their brightly coloured Harley-Davidson scooters, this would dilute the Harley-Davidson brand image to a significant extent.

Research has shown that a product with a considerably different proposition only undermines a brand if it is technically very similar to the flagship product of the brand (see Table 3.1). In the Mona case outlined in Box 3.2, Vifit can be compared with the fictional Harley-Davidson scooter, a product that is perceptually quite close to the flagship product (Mona's desserts and Harley-Davidson's motorcycles) but seeks to appeal to an essentially different motivation for purchase and/or target group.

BOX 3.3 HARLEY-DAVIDSON

The Harley-Davidson brand is slapped not only on motorcycles, but also on cigarettes, beer, aftershave, crayons, almonds and coffee. The brand image that Harley-Davidson adds to these products can be described as 'masculine' and 'macho'. Following on from this associative pattern, a relatively cheap line of aftershaves for men under the same name could intuitively harm the Harley-Davidson brand image. But research has shown that extensions in a wholly different product class than the brand's most stereotypical product (flagship product) hardly have any bearing on the strength of the brand image. Harley-Davidson's most stereotypical product is the motorcycle (the brand's flagship product). The aforementioned research implies that Harley-Davidson aftershave would not, or would hardly, affect the Harley-Davidson brand image for its bikes, simply because consumers are well aware of the fact that there is no common ground between aftershave and motorcycles.

TABLE 3.1 Possible danger of dilution of flagship product brand image caused by other products[8]

	Small distance to flagship product	*Large distance to flagship product*
Small difference in proposition with respect to flagship product	No danger	No danger
Large difference in proposition with respect to flagship product	Great danger of brand dilution	No danger

If one brand markets different products with great differences in proposition and with a small distance between them, you should seriously consider carving the products that differ from the flagship product out of the brand and market them as a separate brand. The question you will have to answer after having made this decision is whether the new brand is financially feasible.

On the basis of criteria relating to contents, you can ascertain whether the products of one brand should be split up into two (or more) brands. The

64 Brand architecture (Step 2)

question is whether this is financially feasible. On the basis of experience, you can assess what it would cost to launch and maintain a new brand. This amount is mainly determined by the extent of media expenses, i.e. advertising on radio and TV. These costs would double for two brands, and triple for three. A provider can decide to keep certain products under one brand after all, simply because the company lacks the financial means to exploit several brands and the projected turnover per brand will not generate enough income to cover the necessary investments. Note that this decision will have far-reaching consequences for the positioning of a brand product. If you are forced to market several different products under one brand, your positioning will inevitably constitute a rather general noncommittal claim. On the other hand, if you are able to market these products under separate brand names, positioning can be a lot more targeted.

The final factor in the decision-making process surrounding the splitting up of a brand into several brands is of a strategic nature. Financial reasons can lead you to conclude that launching a second brand would not be a responsible move, but strategic reasons and projections could then still twist your arm and lead you to launch a second brand after all. At Mona in 1998, projections pointed at continued growth in the market for yoghurt drinks

(previous page) such as Vifit (prebiotic nutrition), and at competitors also jumping on this bandwagon en masse. The brand Yakult had already entered the European market in 1994, and in that year also Danone Actimel (known as DanActive in the USA and Canada) was introduced. Reasons of competition did eventually lead the management of Mona deciding to invest in the market by launching a separate brand (Vifit).

It was at the time quite difficult for Mona to introduce that second brand; the going trend at most companies was one of 'less is more'. In 2001 Vifit was introduced as a separate brand after all. After that it became easier to position the Mona brand clearly, namely as the desserts brand that provides indulgence. Vifit was also better able to create a clear profile in the market after splitting from Mona; Optimel even became a third brand later. This carve-out operation proved to be very successful; in the period 2001–2010 the yearly turnover of the three brands tripled.

The growing importance of the price dimension

Recent years have seen a number of shifts in emphasis in the makeup of brand portfolios, with consequences for brand positioning. We will explain further this using the Brand Portfolio Model (BPM) shown in Figure 3.3.

Unilever's segmentation idea often used to be taken as a textbook example of a brand portfolio. In the margarine market, this company exploited a range of different margarine and cooking fat brands, each targeting a specific consumer segment. Wherever possible, Unilever deployed a separate brand for each discernible market segment. In those days, brand portfolios were all about accumulating 'premium brands' – brands charged with emotional or rational sales arguments through advertising, enabling them to justify a

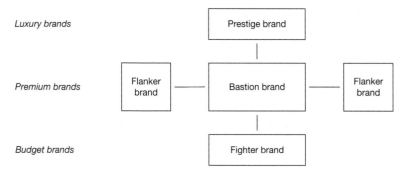

FIGURE 3.3 The Brand Portfolio Model[9]

premium price in the market (i.e. a higher price than a brand with a lesser reputation). Large companies mainly exploited several premium brands in one and the same market. Each of these brands appealed to different wishes and needs, with the company's most profitable brand (the bastion brand) shielded from competing brands by the company's other brands. In terms of the BPM, you can conclude that competition was in those days mainly concentrated on the level of premium brands, i.e. the BPM's *horizontal* dimension.

At the end of the 1990s, the emphasis in brand portfolio building shifted from the horizontal to the *vertical* dimension, i.e. the price dimension in the BPM. This was down to various factors. First, introducing and maintaining brands had become a lot more costly as a result of the media explosion described in Chapter 1. The increase in the number of media outlets made it a financially irresponsible move to target niches with premium brands. Unilever seriously cut back its portfolio from 1600 to 400 brands, with only brands that could actually generate funds to cover the required media expenses making the cut (see Box 3.4). Another factor triggering the shift to the price dimension was the creation of the single European market. Two aspects of that development play a role here: freedom of movement of goods and people, as well as the development of uniform product standards. This is causing national providers to have to compete with non-national providers.

The price dimension is clearly gaining ground in the building of brand portfolios. BMW, for example, branched out into a lower price range by exploiting the Mini brand, and into a higher price range with the Rolls-Royce brand. And remember the example of Renault, endorsing the cheaper brand of car, Dacia.

Brand portfolio and positioning

We have already hinted at the relation between building a brand portfolio and the positioning of the individual brands in that portfolio. You can now draw the following conclusions:

- Exploiting several brands requires clear harmonization of individual brand propositions (positioning then requires a broader outlook than just customer wishes and needs).
- When an organization has several brands, individual brand positioning can be more targeted, because each brand can target specific wishes and needs and/or target groups.

BOX 3.4 UNILEVER'S PATH TO GROWTH

The most eye-catching example of brand portfolio rationalization in recent years is provided by Unilever. In February 2000 the group announced its 'path to growth' strategy. The idea behind this plan was to generate growth in sales and raise operational margins on its remaining brands by reducing the number of brands (from about 1600 to 400). Brands were axed on the basis of three criteria: business strategy fit (does the brand fit into the business strategy?), media exploitation (does the brand have sufficient market share to be able to generate funds to cover required media expenses?), and portfolio balance (how does the brand in question relate to other brands in the portfolio?). After answering these questions, 40 'core global brands' were selected to form the showpieces of Unilever's new strategy. Alongside these core brands, Unilever pinpointed 160 regional or local brands that had to help the company to keep growing (the so-called 'local jewels'). Many of the other brands qualified for delisting. Although the path to growth strategy did not contribute sufficiently to the growth of Unilever as a whole, the following positive outcome was registered:

- Sales share of leading global brands rose from 75 per cent in 1999 to 93 per cent in 2003.
- In 2004 Unilever managed 12 brands – such as Becel/Flora, Blue Band, Dove, Knorr, Lipton, Lux and Rexona – with individual sales figures of over €1 billion (in 1999 only four of the company's brands managed these kinds of figures). In 2007 these 12 brands were responsible for half of Unilever's total turnover.

- Differences between the product propositions can lead to a brand becoming unable to stand out in the market. That is particularly the case when there are differences between products from the same product group.

More than ever, each brand requires a more clearly demarcated pricing level. As competition is mainly concentrated on price, brands can no longer afford to work with great differences in prices or value ratios. For example, although the absolute retail prices of BMW 1, 3, 5 and 7 series cars do indeed differ, all these models are relatively expensive in relation to similar models by other brands. You could therefore say that BMW works with an unambiguous pricing policy.

3.4 Sub-branding

The third branch of brand architecture is sub-branding. This strategy refers to the use of sub-brands alongside product brands. An example is the sub-brand Venus, as in Gillette Venus. Sub-brand names can, as with product brand names, vary from reasonably descriptive to fictitious names. But the common trend is for sub-brands to use a reasonably descriptive name – more so than with product brands. This is down to the fact that sub-brands have to get the proposition of the product in question across right away. This proposition will then concern a unique product feature or benefit that is communicated through the sub-brand. Sub-brands are sometimes a proper brand name with differentiating power, and at other times they are very descriptive. We do not consider nondescript type numbers to be sub-brands.

The use of sub-brands under a product brand offers a range of advantages.[10] The principal advantage is probably that several products can use the name and reputation of the product brand. If the umbrella product brand name is used for all to see in all communication, then all of its sub-brands take advantage of the brand awareness generated by the product brand. A good example of this is offered by Coca-Cola, with sub-brands such as Cherry, Light (in some countries known as Diet Coke) and Zero (see Box 3.5),

---

BOX 3.5 COCA-COLA ZERO POSITIONING

Coca-Cola Zero was first launched in Spain in 2006. It was introduced because market research had shown that men did not identify with the Coca-Cola Light proposition. Coca-Cola Zero is intended for men who are looking for exquisite taste, but without the sugar. Coca-Cola devised the Zero proposition to appeal to men with a carefree lifestyle, with all the good things that entails, without having to settle for anything less (i.e. compromising on taste). The Zero message is therefore 'Great life without downsides'. In order to make this message hit home with the target group, Coca-Cola looked into their passions. In some countries these were identified as racing and gaming. Based on these drives, Coca-Cola subsequently set up targeted marketing communication campaigns for the Zero target group.

alongside the flagship product Coca-Cola regular. As a result, new products can be launched relatively easily under a strong product brand.

One last point we have to make on the use of sub-brands is that they should ideally evoke a 'series idea'. This is particularly clear in the case of makes of car: Volkswagen, for example, has a history of using (corrupted) names of winds as the names of its models, such as Bora, Jetta, Passat, Scirocco and Vento. Consumers will often sense that such names come under one and the same main brand name. In practice, sub-branding often uses both brand names and descriptive labels. An example is Nivea, whose extensions Vital and Visage have more of a brand status than labels such as For Men, Sun, Soft, Crème, Body, Hand, Hair Care, Bath Care, and Deodorant.

Implications for positioning

The name of a sub-brand can be used underneath a product brand name. Sub-branding is an obvious option especially in the case of a broad brand. By using different names for individual propositions, you can create a clear-cut proposition that anticipates certain wishes and needs and/or identifies clear target groups. As there is often no budget to properly charge sub-brands through advertising, the name itself has to be a first indicator of the sub-brand's proposition. These kinds of brands are therefore often referred to as 'proposition brands'. The name Vital – as a sub-brand of Nivea – lets potential users know that it is a product to keep the skin young and lively, primarily intended for 'mature skin'. Where positioning is concerned, sub-brands are mainly intended to communicate the proposition to the outside world; the product brand above the sub-brands will then be the puller claiming more general associations or an emotional value.

3.5 Brand architecture conclusions

This chapter has maintained a clear distinction between three brand levels: corporate brands, product brands and sub-brands. In Section 3.2 we dealt with the choice that an organization has to make to either market its corporate name or launch one or several product brands. In practice, companies tend to use one of two brand levels:

- a corporate brand with one or several product brands (Yamaha WaveRunner);
- a product brand with one or several sub-brands (Gillette Venus).

Some organizations have opted to deploy all three brand levels. This often leads to propositions that are hard to grasp for customers. The division above makes the point that both options leave room to pursue a positioning difference between brands. When choosing a corporate brand with one or several product brands, the former can be given a more emotional look and feel, with the product brand taking care of functional and instrumental attraction. The same goes for a product brand with one or several sub-brands: the product brand can be given a more emotional look and feel, with the sub-brands taking care of functional and instrumental attraction. Both situations require well-considered choices, which are, in turn, conducive to targeted positioning of the brands in question.

This chapter wraps up the internal analysis part of the positioning process. In the following two chapters, we will deal with the external analysis needed for positioning. In Chapter 4 we will discuss target group analysis (Step 3 from the positioning roadmap) and in Chapter 5 competitor analysis (Step 4). But before we start focusing on external aspects, we will summarize the main points of Steps 1 and 2 in Checklist 1.

Notes

1. Sullivan (1990); Simonin and Ruth (1998).
2. See Kapferer (2001, Chapter 1) on 'the convergence of brand cultures'.
3. DelVecchio (2000).
4. Laforet and Saunders (1994, 1999, 2005).
5. Gürhan-Canli and Maheswaran (1998); Roedder John et al. (1998).
6. Brown and Dacin (1997).
7. For an overview on negative and positive purchase motivations, see Rossiter and Bellman (2005, Chapter 8).
8. Source: Riezebos (2003, p. 227).
9. Source: Riezebos (2003, p. 197).
10. Milberg et al. (1997).

CHECKLIST 1

Summary of the internal analysis

In Chapters 2 and 3 we have covered the internal analysis as part of the positioning process. In the following we list the main steps from this analysis in a convenient checklist. This will provide you with a quick source of reference for the compilation of organization-related information.

Corporate identity

1 Make a note of a few important aspects of the organization's history, such as:

   a) Who founded the company, and what were their founding principles (what objectives did the founders pursue by setting up the organization)?
   b) What important milestones has the organization achieved in its past, and why are these events still remembered?
   c) Who are considered 'heroes' in the organization's history, and why?
   d) What stories are told internally about the organization, and what is the deeper meaning behind these stories?
   e) Did the organization ever go through a crisis, and how was that situation handled?

2 Try to put your finger on the organization's drive, i.e. whether it targets control or flexibility, and whether the organization is more a closed or an open system:

   a) Determine on the basis of these dimensions whether the organization is product-oriented, process-oriented, market-oriented or organization-oriented (see Checklist Table 1.1).

CHECKLIST TABLE 1.1

Open

	Market-oriented:	Organization-oriented:	
	• 'They'-oriented • Core competencies: market knowledge, customer contact • Weak vision–strong mission • Performance culture	• 'We'-oriented • Core competencies: employee motivation, collaboration • Strong vision–strong mission • Adhocracy	
Control			Flexibility
	Process-oriented:	Product-oriented:	
	• 'It'-oriented • Core competencies: internal and external logistics • Weak vision–weak mission • Formal culture	• 'I'-oriented • Core competencies: innovation, production • Strong vision–weak mission • Family culture	

Closed

b) Pinpoint two core competencies of the organization. Choose from the following: innovation, production, internal logistics, external logistics, market knowledge, customer contact, employee motivation, and collaboration.

c) Be as objective as possible in defining whether the organization's vision is a strong or a weak one (criterion: does it paint a clear picture of expected market developments?). And also ascertain with equal objectivity whether the organization has a strong or a weak mission statement. (Criterion: does it mention concrete objectives and does it aim high enough?) Take stock of employees' commitment to the purport of the vision and mission statement (thought), of whether employees actually feel touched by it (feeling), and of whether they feel encouraged to act in line with the mission statement (action).

3 Describe the organization's culture and try to indicate which corporate culture type is dominant: family culture, formal culture, performance culture or adhocracy.

4 Identify the corporate and customer values as valid implicitly within the organization. Do so by completing Checklist Table 1.2 for the listed target groups: employees, investors, government/media/special interest groups/suppliers/general public, and (potential) customers.

CHECKLIST TABLE 1.2

		Corporate values			*Customer values*
Who	Employees	Investors	Government/ media/special interest groups/ suppliers/ general public		(Potential) customers
What	Quality Service Innovation Success	Value Growth Profit	Environmental awareness Sustainable Social contribution		Simplicity Health Sustainability
How	Customer- driven Respectful Result- driven Enterprising	Reliable Aggressive	Responsible Ethical Committed Transparent		Convenience Closeness Security

Brand architecture

1 In terms of brand-name strategy: identify the brand the organization will be marketing. Corporate brand and/or product brand(s)? Take stock of the propositions of these brands.
2 In terms of brand portfolio:
   a) Use the Brand Portfolio Model (BPM; see Figure 3.4) to chart how the organization's brands relate to each other (bastion, fighter, flanker or prestige brand).
   b) Use the flowchart (see Checklist Figure 1.1) to check whether certain product combinations can or cannot be marketed under the same brand name.

74 Checklist 1

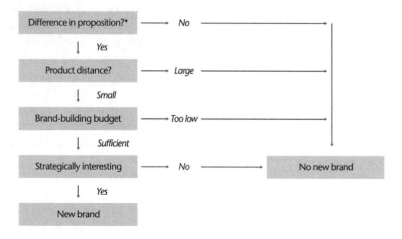

CHECKLIST FIGURE 1.1

* Consider, for example, differences in perceived corporate ability, differences between the products in reasons for buying, highly divergent pricing propositions, different levels of sensitivity to commerciality, or differences between target groups.

3   In terms of sub-branding: take stock of the sub-brands in use, identify the degree of descriptiveness of the names in use, and define the correlation between these sub-brands.

4
TARGET GROUP ANALYSIS (STEP 3)

In Chapters 2 and 3 we analysed the *internal* environment of the brand that is being positioned, covering the corporate identity and the brand architecture. In this fourth chapter we will start on the analysis of the *external* environment. This analysis is also twofold. This chapter focuses on the first step of the external analysis: target group analysis (the third step of the pre-positioning analysis). In Chapter 5 we will deal with the second step of the external analysis: competitor analysis. The concept of 'target group' in this context should be taken quite broadly. Apart from establishing a positioning in the eyes of customers, an organization can also position itself in a certain way in the labour market or as a socially responsible organization for the general public. In Figure 4.1 the target group of the positioned brand is captured in the left circle of the BTC model.

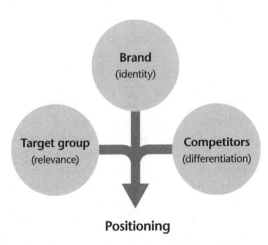

FIGURE 4.1 Target group as part of the external analysis of a positioning process

In Chapter 1 we dealt with the relevance of positioning. We pointed out that positioning is essential for any provider, simply because it is getting ever more difficult to find an empty spot in the chock-a-block minds of the target group members. Just consider the fact that the Trade Marks and Designs Registration Office of the European Union has over 1 million brands on its books, while our brain is 'only' estimated to contain about 4000 brands.[1] This means that the majority of all registered trade marks never make it into our consciousness.

In Chapter 1 we also focused on the different mind shares brands have managed to obtain (see Box 1.3 about Coca-Cola versus Pepsi-Cola). In order to achieve good brand positioning, we need knowledge on how our brains store brand-related information. This chapter will therefore first go into what has come to be known as 'mind management'. Section 4.1 will outline the latest insights and trends in that area. Section 4.2 will subsequently describe a method (means–end chain analysis) that ascertains 'what' the target group considers important, and in particular 'why' that is important to them. This analysis forms an important basis for brand positioning, and the extent to which that ties in with the way brand information is stored in our minds. Section 4.3 will briefly summarize this chapter.

4.1 Mind management

Psychologists have posited that a brand is represented by a network of interconnected memory nodes in our minds.[2] The central node in this network is the one where the brand name is stored. Whenever a consumer is confronted with a brand name, not only is the central memory node activated, but so too are the other (peripheral) memory nodes networked to that central node.[3] Connections between the central memory node and peripheral nodes make up a network of associations. This network of associations is referred to as a *brand schema* (sometimes also called a *brand engram*).[4]

Aside from the brand name, a brand schema contains three other types of nodes: product class, attributes and values. We will illustrate this via the beer brand Budweiser. The first association of consumers with Budweiser will be 'beer'. The brand is foremost connected to a product class. When asked to give further associations with the Budweiser brand, consumers will possibly come up with the nodes 'companionship' and 'American'. These are associations with attributes that can be divided into concrete attributes ('American') and benefits of beer consumption ('companionship'). Another association will be 'friendship', because this 'value' is consequently stressed in Budweiser brand communication.

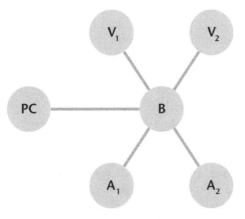

FIGURE 4.2 Diagram of the different memory nodes in a brand schema

Figure 4.2 presents the different memory nodes in a diagram:

- The central memory node B represents the brand name.
- The memory node PC represents the association with the product class.
- The memory nodes A_1 and A_2 represent the associations with attributes.
- The memory nodes V_1 and V_2 represent the values a brand appeals to.

Many of the brands in our mind are related to one product class. But there are exceptions: the name Michelin, for example, is related to the product class car tyres as well as to the red hotel and restaurant guide, and the brand name Virgin evokes quite a number of different product classes. To keep things manageable, we will limit ourselves in this text to brands that are related to one product class. The central memory node of the brand (B) is generally associated with several attributes (A), and ideally also with a few values (V). Attributes can also be linked to a value. In the following sub-sections we will further flesh out each of the three following connections within a brand schema: brand and product class, brand and attributes, and brand and values.

Brand–product class connection

Consumers get to grips with the deluge of information in the world around them by splitting it up into groups or categories. This process is called *categorization*.[5] A category is a collection of people or objects with one or several common features or functions. In our day-to-day existence we are continuously trying to categorize the things we observe in order not to be overwhelmed by the complexity of our surroundings. On holiday, for example, we might try to spot fellow countrymen by their clothing, behaviour and hairstyle. And when confronted with an animal type we are not familiar with, we attempt to assess whether the animal in question poses a danger on the basis of certain features.

The benefit of categorization is that we will not have to go through an elaborate assessment process for everyone and everything we encounter. That is how simple decision-making rules come about – also referred to as 'heuristics'. Category information contains simple decision-making rules that help ascertain whether something or someone comes under a certain category or not. And if it does, we immediately ascribe all sorts of stereotypical characteristics to the object or person in question. We tend to think of fat people as convivial, for example, and can tell by someone's hair whether he or she is casual or not. Brands are also subject to this phenomenon: we generally consider German cars reliable and praise Italian products for their design.

In the case of brands, we look at a limited number of features to assess whether they belong in a certain product class or not. A four-wheeled object with a combustion engine and a steering wheel is quickly classified as a car. But the importance of these features can change over time. Cars with an electric engine used to not be considered 'proper' cars, but the success of hybrids has lowered the relevance of engine type in the assessment of whether an object is classified as a car or not.

We spend every day of our lives categorizing our observations. The downside of categorization is that it sometimes causes us to gloss over things, leading to half-hearted assessments. The categorization process also leads us to automatically foist certain characteristics on a product or situations, whereas these may not even apply. A well-known example of such behaviour is provided by an experiment that saw students called to their professor's office, where they subsequently had to wait to participate in a research project. After waiting about five minutes, and after having left the office, they were asked to describe what they had seen in the office. Many of the students said they had seen books, although these had actually been removed for the purposes of the experiment. As it turned out, our brains are conditioned to perceive books in a professor's office.[6]

In the opposite case, our brains reject information if we are unable to categorize it, which has far-reaching consequences. An example is the perception of the BMW C1, a 'motorcycle' with a roof, a safety cage, a

windscreen wiper and a safety belt, which was introduced in 2000 (above). Partly due to the fact that a helmet was not obligatory for this vehicle, real bikers did not categorize the BMW C1 as a motorcycle. The C1 was axed in 2003. BMW could have made the C1 a success if it had come up with a separate category for it – such as 'scoot car' – and put that category on consumers' mind map. However, such a strategy requires a hefty communication budget.

Another example of a brand product that failed to establish an instantly recognizable link to the intended product class was Pepsi's 7-Up Ice Cola (overleaf), which was launched in 1995. This concoction was a carbonated cola-flavoured drink. But it was not cola-coloured, it was clear, just like regular 7-Up. Consumers simply did not know what it was – cola is brown and 7-Up is clear. The colour of the beverage did not dovetail with the information contained in the memory node for this product class. This product would have had a greater chance of success if Pepsi had not tried to present a unique colour for this 'cola', or if they had come up with a new category name for the product.

The idea behind brand positioning is to claim attributes that set the brand off from competing brands.[7] These are referred to as the 'points of difference'

(PODs).[8] These unique attributes can be used in all communication centred on the brand as unique selling propositions (USPs), providing they are relevant to the target group. USPs or 'exclusive sales arguments' tend to provide the pull that leads people to purchase the product in question. But alongside these unique attributes, it is also important to share certain attributes with competitors, simply in order to ensure that consumers can place the brand product in a product category and know what need it fills. These common attributes for the product category are called 'points of parity' (POPs). POPs can be traced by asking the target group which attributes they feel go with a certain product class, and what the relative importance of each of the listed attributes is.

The above observations serve to further flesh out Figure 4.2: not only the memory node of a brand name can be connected to associations with attributes (and values), but so can the memory node of the product class in question. In line with the difference between POPs and PODs, you can say that POP associations are linked to the product class node and that POD associations are linked to the node of the brand in question (see Figure 4.3). Positioning entails finding out which associations belong in the realm of the POP domain and which in the realm of the POD.

As part of the relation between PODs and POPs there is also the MAYA principle ('most advanced yet acceptable') to consider, which was devised by Raymond Loewy, an influential 20th-century industrial designer.[9] This principle states that a product has to be sufficiently different to attract consumers' attention ('most advanced'). But too much differentiation leads to consumers failing to link the product to a product class. That means that a product also always has to be recognizable as part of a certain product category ('yet acceptable').

Despite innovating brand products running the risk of losing touch with a product class, there are also examples of brand products that managed to break through the categorization process into product classes. Fresh fruit juices provide one example. Brands such as Tropicana (Pepsico) and Minute Maid (Coca-Cola Company) stress the freshness of their juices by placing them in the chilled section at the supermarket, amidst dairy products, and even using cartons that were traditionally only used for milk. Tropicana and Minute Maid claim ultimate freshness, but in recent years their position has been undermined by the rise of smoothies, especially those marketed by

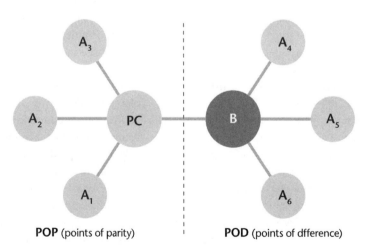

FIGURE 4.3 POP (points of parity) versus POD (points of difference) associations

Innocent Drinks, which has changed consumers' frame of reference for fresh fruit juices. Smoothies have deflected consumers' freshness perception onto themselves. This has eventually led to Tropicana launching its own smoothies and, in 2009, to The Coca-Cola Company participating in Innocent Drinks.

Sometimes a brand (or person) is 'pigeonholed' to such an extent that it simply gets stuck in that category.[10] Atari, for example, never managed to make it out of the gaming consoles market. People can also suffer from a stereotypical categorization. It took John Travolta 20 years to wash off the image of 'Tony Manero', the character he played in the enormously successful film *Saturday Night Fever* in 1977.

Brand–attributes connection

In this section we will zoom in on the connection between the brand and the associations with certain attributes. There are basically two types of attributes: product features and product benefits. Before delving into the connection between the brand and associations with these attributes, we will first focus on one special brand attribute, namely the logo.

Logos are stored in our brains in a 'holistic' manner. That means that we do not subject them to a thorough analysis before storing them in our brains, but only process them on the basis of a rough outline. A logo can help target group members to *remember* the brand names of lesser-known brands.[11] For better-known brands, the logo is mainly a brand identifier. McDonald's golden arches logo is a good example of an effective brand identifier. Even young children who have not yet learned to speak can recognize the brand on the basis of this logo.

The logo is only one of the attributes to which a brand name can be linked in our minds. Well-known brands evoke associations with several attributes; these attributes can, in turn, call forth concrete product features and/or expected product benefits. The term 'features' has to be taken quite broadly here; a 'country of origin' can also be classed as a product feature. You should bear in mind that this is all about perception; it may very well be that a brand evokes an association with a specific product feature that in actual fact it does not have at all. Many Americans, for example, think Heineken is a German brand because of the German-sounding name. There is, however, no need for the Dutch beer brand Heineken to start negating this association – partly because 'Germany' conjures up a string of positive connotations where beer is concerned.

As we have said, attributes can be split up into product features and product benefits. *Product features* include shape, colour, options, price, packaging and brand name. Services are often made more tangible by communication and behaviour. This makes communication and behaviour also perceivable as product features. Take the way in which queries are dealt with by a call centre, for example, or the way staff members are dressed. For retailers, product features can include features such as shop decoration and layout, as well as the assortment on offer. *Product benefits* follow directly from product features. One feature of the Sun dishwashing tablet is that its wrapping dissolves, leading to the product benefit that you don't have to touch the tablet itself (many people wash their hands right away after handling a dishwashing tablet). A biscuit's product feature 'made with butter' can lead to the perception that it will have a 'fuller taste' (a product benefit in terms of taste).

Where the connection between brand name and associations with attributes (product features and product benefits) is concerned, it is important to distinguish the following three aspects:[12]

- the contents of the association;
- the valency of the association (positive or negative);
- the strength of the link between the association and the brand.

The first point, the *contents* of an association, literally refers to the content consumers associate with a brand name. That is generally quite easy to find out by asking people what ideas they have about a certain brand. For example, the Alfa Romeo brand triggers associations including sporty, Italian, distinguishing, unconventional and, to a lesser extent, rust-prone (which was a problem 15–20 years ago).

Apart from the actual content, the *valency* of an association is also relevant. Valency is the extent to which an association makes a positive or negative contribution to the brand image. Continuing the Alfa Romeo example, the associations sporty, Italian, distinguishing and unconventional will have a positive value for most consumers. However, the association 'rust-prone' has a highly negative charge. A brand manager will, of course, want his brand to evoke as many positive and as few negative associations as possible. Research has shown that denying negative associations is a futile exercise – it actually has the opposite effect. It is a much better idea to 'reframe' a negative association, making its valency positive.[13] Or one could state that the cause of the negative association is no longer in play. In the case of Alfa Romeo, car production initially used much more recycled steel, which is more rust-prone.

The *strength* of an association refers to the question of how rigidly the association is tied to a brand name. This can usually be ascertained by looking at the order in which consumers list associations. For Alfa Romeo that order will probably be 'sporty'–'Italian'–'rust-prone'. The bond of the association 'sporty' with the brand is probably a lot stronger than that of the association 'rust-prone' (although it was probably the other way round 15–20 years ago). The strongest associations with attributes most likely come about through direct experiences with a product. Word-of-mouth advertising will subsequently generate strong associations. Advertising generally only leads to relatively weak associations, because of its low credibility. But high-quality targeted advertising that pushes the right buttons in consumers will achieve more than random advertising communications with maximum exposure. Consistency is also an important factor in determining the strength of an association. Consumers detest confusion; diverging messages and experiences severely weaken a product's or brand's position. This once again underlines the importance of not shying away from making targeted choices.

Figure 4.4 reflects the connection between the brand name and the associations with attributes in diagrammatic form. In this fictitious example the brand (B) is associated with three attributes: A_1, A_2 and A_3. The strength of the bond between the association and the brand is reflected in the length of the lines. Attribute A_1 is most often associated with the brand, followed by attributes A_2 and A_3. Valency is depicted by a plus or minus sign in this figure. Attributes A_1 and A_2 make a positive contribution to the brand image;

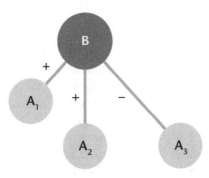

FIGURE 4.4 Three aspects of association in a diagram: content, valency and strength

attribute A_3 a negative one. Applying this figure to the Alfa Romeo brand, A_1 could in terms of content represent 'sporty' and A_2 'Italian design'. In the situation painted in this example, consumers associate Alfa Romeo more strongly with 'sporty' than with 'Italian design'; nonetheless, both associations make a positive contribution to the brand image. A_3 would in that case represent 'rust-prone', a negatively charged association that people make less quickly than those of 'sporty' and 'Italian design'.

Within any positioning analysis, listing the associative ties between a brand and its attributes is always helpful.[14] Which attribute associations does the brand evoke (content)? Do these associations reflect positively or negatively on the brand (valency)? How strongly is the association linked to the brand (strength)? This is relatively easy to research: by asking which associations a brand evokes, and recording the order in which associations are given, you can get an idea of the content and strength of the associations (associations mentioned first tend to be more closely tied to the brand than those listed later). And by subsequently asking whether an association is a positive or a negative factor in the valuation of the brand, you can determine the valency of the associations mentioned.

Brand–values connection

A value is a long-term goal that people pursue throughout their lives. In principle, a value is independent of the product and the situation. Values are fixed – more or less constant – ideas about what people consider important in their lives. Strong brands distinguish themselves from weaker ones because they manage to claim one or several values. Whenever a brand manager succeeds in coupling his brand to one or several values in the minds of his target group members, the brand will be experienced as a meaningful one.

Values can manifest themselves on three levels:

- On the level of fundamental needs, such as eating, drinking and sleeping, but also of safety and convenience. Volkswagen, for example, has spent a long time stressing the reliability of its products, while Volvo has claimed safety.
- On the level of social needs, such as wanting to fit in and the need for respect and appreciation. Vodafone's communication always highlights the social aspects, and Nokia does that same in a more literal fashion with its pay-off 'Connecting people'.
- On the level of personal needs, such as intellectual stimulation. A literal example of this personal appeal is HP's 'The computer is personal again.'

86 Target group analysis (Step 3)

A raft of different lists of values have been compiled in marketing circles over the years. One of the best-known ones is the Rokeach Value Survey (RVS) by Milton Rokeach;[15] we have summarized his list of 18 terminal values in Table 4.1 by grouping them on the three abovementioned levels.

Apart from these terminal values, Rokeach also identifies instrumental values. These represent behavioural characteristics that people think highly of, such as courageous, cheerful, loving and capable. Appendix B contains a more recent and extensive list of Rokeach's terminal and instrumental values.

One important issue that has to be addressed when positioning a brand is how a value can be linked to the brand. We will go into this using the diagram presented in Figure 4.5. In this example the brand in question evokes two

TABLE 4.1 The 18 terminal values of the Rokeach Value Survey, classified in three categories

Fundamental needs	Social needs	Personal needs
Freedom	Mature love	Self-respect
National security	Friendship	Equality
Peace	Comfort	Beauty
Pleasure	Happiness	Wisdom
Excitement	Sense of accomplishment	Inner harmony
Family security	Social recognition	Salvation

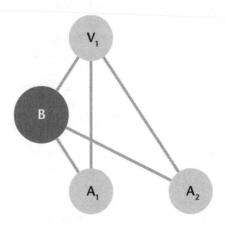

FIGURE 4.5 Connections between brand, value(s) and attributes

associations with attributes and one association with a value. This brand has the option to emphasize the value association by explicitly naming this value in all advertising. But the chances are that the viewer or reader will not catch on to the relevance of the value in relation to the brand because proof of such relevance is not provided. The first lesson to learn from that is that a value has to be relevant to both the target group and the brand product. The latter means that a value should be tied not only to the brand in question, but also to one or several of the attributes that the brand is associated with. Volvo made the value 'safety' relevant by drawing attention to attributes such as the safety cage concept and ABS. This also included looking into how attributes that are not visible to the naked eye could be brought to the fore. The story goes that Volvo purposely kept the designs of its cars a little boxy to stress the presence of the safety cage. A value should preferably be linked to several attributes (see Figure 4.5). Strong brands are not only associated with relevant values, but also captured in a complex mind map with more cross-connections than weaker brands. The second lesson to be learnt here is that values do not necessarily need to be made explicit. Having a target group experience values indirectly (through the highlighting of certain attributes) can help build an equally strong, if not stronger, mind map around the brand as when advertising constantly tries to pound home certain values.

From the perspective of mind management, it would be helpful to reiterate that strong brands are the ones that have managed to claim values that possess a certain meaning for one or several attributes, and that strong brands have often implanted a more extensive brand schema in the brains of their target group members than weaker brands. The extent of a brand schema is reflected not only in the number of associations, but also in the mutual cross-connections between associations (attributes in the way of features and benefits, and/or values). The question now is how to use above information to build a strong brand. The following section will go some way towards answering that question by providing a method that helps you grasp the means–end chain of a brand, as well as the composition of a means–end chain for the product category.

4.2 Means–end analysis

Before dealing with the method for the mapping of a means–end chain for a product category and a brand, we will first cover target group selection as part of the positioning process, because if you decide to select several target groups, you will have to run the method described in the subsequent section for all these different target groups. The next section focuses on the essence of the means–end analysis: the so-called 'means–end chains'. In Section 4.2.3 we will subsequently discuss a number of techniques for the formation of such means–end chains.

Target group selection

As we have already mentioned at different points in this book, positioning is not limited to the target group consumers or customers. Brand positioning can be aimed at different target groups. In Table 4.2 we have included a list of target groups divided into four categories: human resources management (HRM), financial, marketing and 'licence to operate'. HRM includes employees, as well as their family members, who play an important role in the background (motivation, showing understanding for working overtime, and the like). But the labour market at large is also an important target group from the perspective of HRM. It can also include employers' federations and trade unions, as well as the company's own staff participation council. From a financial point of view, target groups can comprise, apart from banks and credit institutions, shareholders, investment firms and the financial press. The latter is a particularly important target group for listed companies. In marketing terms, target groups are customers, or other companies using or consuming (end-customers) the products of the company, as well as parties in the distribution sector between the company and the end-customer. In the

TABLE 4.2 Different target groups for brand positioning, divided into four categories

Category	Target group
HRM	Employees
	Labour market: current
	Labour market: potential (students)
	Employers' federations and trade unions
Financial	Banks and credit institutions
	Shareholders, investment firms
	Financial press
Marketing	End-customers (companies, consumers)
	Direct channels, intermediaries (trade parties and the like)
Licence to operate	Local and provincial authorities
	(Inter)national political figures
	Media
	Special interest and lobby groups, NGOs

case of goods the latter can be a wholesaler or retailer, and in the case of products involving a substantial financial transaction it can be an intermediary or estate agent. Finally, a target group that should not be overlooked is the one made up by those parties that influence an organization's 'licence to operate'. Organizations can only function when they are not constantly being questioned. The livestock, fish farming and fishing industries are all industries that regularly receive bad press. Companies active in these sectors are constantly required to demonstrate how animal-friendly and responsible their operations are – not only to the authorities, but also to special interest and lobby groups, such as NGOs.[16] Positioning can help these industries make that positive message stick.

It is, of course, very possible that other target groups not listed in Table 4.2 are conceivable for specific markets and/or specific brands. At a later stage, it may be necessary to designate sub-target groups within a target group for you to aim your communication at.

Means–end chains

Means–end analysis is a method that will help you find out how to turn concrete attributes of a product or service into abstract values, and how to then convert these values into attributes in concrete customer contacts. Means–end theory starts from the given that people give meaning to everything they see, hear, etc. That meaning is subsequently stored in existing mental schemata (categorized). It is a kind of stereotyping or pigeon-holing, simply to keep personal relations manageable. But what we are focusing on here is the meaning you ascribe to products and brands, i.e. your assessment of how specific products and brands can be a means to an end, with that end being the values you seek to uphold or realize. The spiritual fathers of means–end analysis are Thomas J. Reynolds and Jonathan Gutman (see Box 4.1).

By analysing these meanings, and structuring them, you will find yourself able to cleverly lay bare associations surrounding a product category and brand, in order to subsequently try to steer these associations. The appeal of this method lies in the fact that it enables you to establish an associative chain between concrete (product) features and what people consider important (benefits and values). This takes us right into the heart of branding policy: 'How should my brand come across, so that people can infer what it can do for them?' This method not only points you in the right direction where communication is concerned, but also provides pointers for concrete

90 Target group analysis (Step 3)

> ## BOX 4.1 MEANS–END ANALYSIS ACCORDING TO REYNOLDS AND GUTMAN[17]
>
> The term 'means–end analysis' was coined in the works of Reynolds and Gutman (1984). They described the process that consumers run through to put a meaning on product attributes. The basic underlying assumption is that people are not after the product in itself, but rather after the benefits the product offers for them personally. They are after the 'beauty' and 'being admired' thanks to the 'white teeth' and 'fresh breath' achieved by a certain brand of toothpaste. The revolutionary aspect of this theory was that it claimed that consumers make purchase choices on the basis of the meaning that product attributes have to them. If you are a follower of this approach, the brand manager's focus will shift from product attributes to the more abstract meaning these attributes can have for consumers.

customer contacts, such as the way in which customers are assisted by service staff. People base their idea of the brand essence on these contacts. We therefore endorse the adage 'branding is a contact sport'. After all, concrete customer contacts are the instances where it becomes clear whether a brand fulfils its promise.

The actual output of a means–end analysis comes in the shape of 'means–end chains', which are also referred to as 'means–end ladders'.[18] Figure 4.6 depicts the structure of a means–end chain. The chain is made up of three levels, each with two sub-levels:

1   Values or goals:

   a)   terminal values: the values people want to pursue in their lives;
   b)   instrumental values: the way in which people seek to realize the terminal values in their lives.

2   Meanings/consequences:

   a)   psycho-social meanings: the way in which a consumer can use certain product or service features in a psycho-social context;
   b)   functional consequences: the consequences of the use of a product or service for a consumer.

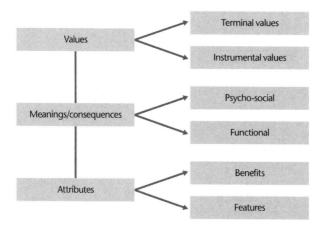

FIGURE 4.6 Means–end chain (ladder)

3   Product or service attributes:
   a) benefits of the use of a product or service;
   b) concrete features of the product or service.

In practice, all six levels rarely converge in one product or brand. A straightforward example of a means–end chain for a product is a crisps brand that has added a specific flavouring to its crisps that leads people to eat less of them (see Figure 4.7). In this example, crisps with a strong taste sensation cause you to cut down on them, making eating crisps less fattening, leading to you maintaining a better figure, which eventually helps boost your self-esteem. This example shows how a brand can link its attributes to values through an associative chain of relevant meanings. The meanings people give to the different attributes are gates to the 'heart' of the target group, and therefore often the central focus point in the positioning of successful brands.

When running a means–end analysis, you can distinguish between means–end chains for a market or product class and means–end chains for a brand within that market. First compiling chains for a market will enable a brand manager to subsequently choose on which chain(s) he wants to base his brand within the chains of the market. So where the brand is concerned, it is all about claiming a specific part of a means–end chain for a market.

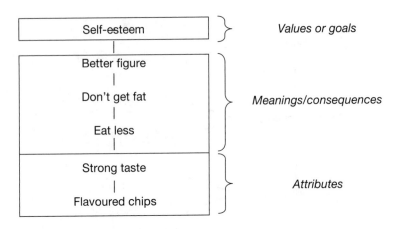

FIGURE 4.7 Example of a means-end chain[19]

© 2001 from *Understanding Consumer Decision Making* by T.J. Reynolds and J. Gutman.

Laddering

Means–end analysis involves interviewing people in your target group. The in-depth interviewing technique developed for this is referred to as 'laddering'.[20] Laddering is based on the 'Why' question: the respondent is asked why a certain feature is important to him, and subsequently why the reason he gave is important to him, etc., etc. The laddering interview can be organized in two different ways:

- using grouping tasks, such as Kelly's repertory grid and natural grouping;
- using direct questions.

Kelly's repertory grid method[21] presents a respondent with three products or three cards with brand names, and then asks him which two he feels make the best match, and why the third one does not fit in. This can be repeated several times (there are three possible matches in this task), always accompanied by the 'why' question. For example: Why do these two brands match, and why does the other not fit in? Why is the distinction you make important to you?

Natural grouping involves more than three products or brand names, making for considerably more possible matches than with the repertory grid (the maximum number of matches in natural grouping depends on the number of products or brand names used).

The method of asking *direct questions* is particularly suited when the target group has little or no awareness of the brands in the category in question. You will then have to ask direct questions about attributes, meanings and values for the product category. This applies for target groups who are not familiar with the product category ('novice target groups'), such as mothers-to-be looking to purchase baby products, or elderly people who are in the market for their first rolling walkers.

Laddering can involve both bottom-up and top-down questioning. Bottom-up questions enable the interviewer to establish which features and/or criteria a respondent considers relevant, and why. With this information you can compile a means–end chain from the bottom up (attributes → meanings → values). Or, as soon as the interviewer has an idea of which values are considered important, he or she can start targeting the question whether and how a value can be realized in practice. This is the top-down line of questioning (values → consequences → attributes). If the values of a brand are already known, the interviewer can start asking top-down questions almost right away. The idea is to find out how a brand can manifest certain values in different customer contacts. The middle level of the bottom-up method usually refers to meanings, as you seek to find out what meaning people give to concrete attributes. At the middle level of the top-down method, on the other hand, you are dealing with consequences, because you want to identify the practical consequences of a choice for a certain value.

Each brand has different 'domains' of customer contacts. A brand of fast-moving consumer goods (FMCG) usually has three: product appearance, marketing communication and any possible after-sales service. Even though brand values have to be constant throughout these three domains, the way in which they come to life in practice does differ. If an FMCG brand, for example, stands for the value 'reliable', this value can be expressed differently on the product's packaging than in marketing communication. Retail formats have more domains to consider than an FMCG brand: product appearance (of the house brand), marketing communication, after-sales service, product range, shop layout and employee behaviour. The means–end analysis can be used to compile a means–end chain for each domain, which, incidentally, makes this method rather labour-intensive.

Means–end analysis is a technique a manager or researcher has to be able to use with a certain level of creativity. On the one hand, the interview may produce an unexpected means–end chain that the interviewer will then have to further explore in subsequent interviews (this requires flexibility and willingness to deviate from any preset line of questioning). On the other hand, creativity is also required because means–end chains sometimes appear to go against the 'laws of logic'. In order to substantiate the above with an example, we will draw on a specific means–end survey that was done for a retail format. One of the values posited in this survey was 'reliability', which was converted into the consequence that the store would not defraud customers and would provide them with value for money. In practice, this value was reflected in sharp-priced own-brand products, a money-back guarantee and no-frills shop fittings. However, in one of the interviews a woman also associated low prices with queues at the checkout (she figured that low prices meant the retailer had to cut checkout staff to stay profitable). In follow-up interviews, this new association was checked further. It soon turned out that more consumers had the same idea of a (not too long) queue at the checkout. Queuing at the checkout is here a customer contact that people turn out to ascribe a certain meaning to.

In Box 4.2 we outline positioning research based on a means–end analysis. The central question here is how secondary school students select the university where they will continue their education. This example describes four steps that you can also run through in positioning research.

BOX 4.2 MEANS–END CHAIN FOR UNIVERSITY SELECTION[22]

The objective of the research was to ascertain what criteria youngsters use in the selection of a higher education institution. Before starting the survey, a clear distinction was established between choosing what to study and choosing where to study. The research focused on the latter question. The study was split up into four steps.

Step 1: Defining the product category

During the interviews it emerged that location limited the competition scope, since the respondents indicated that they wanted to continue to live at home with their parents and study at the nearest suitable university.

Step 2: Defining the product features

Each interview started with the question of which features the respondent considered important in the selection of a university. This led to a

continued . . .

list of features. These features were subsequently arranged in a hierarchy of importance by looking at how often each was mentioned. This can be risky because a feature that is mentioned often may not necessarily be the most important one for the final choice. It is therefore advisable to ask the respondent during the interview to rank the features in order of importance. In this study the following relevant features emerged:

- location: distance, public transport connections;
- institution: name (reputation), size;
- building: atmosphere/image, facilities, size;
- courses: desired course is offered.

Step 3: Laddering in terms of benefits, meanings and values

After defining the features, the study continued by 'laddering' them one by one. It did so by asking the question 'How important is distance to you, and why?' The answers to this question were input at the level of benefits and meanings – for example, 'I consider proximity very important because I'm not intending to move out of my parents' house any time soon.' The benefit of a university that is close by is that the student can continue to live in the parental home. When asked why the respondent preferred to live with his or her parents, the answers were 'to save money' or 'because it's easier that way' (functional meaning).

Step 4: Compiling a means–end chain

After having finished the interviews, the next step was to distract the different means–end chains that together enabled the construction of the full means–end chain structure. This required the grouping of statements. Statements such as 'when others look up to you, your self-esteem grows' and 'I do find it important what others think about me, to have a good job' can, for example, both be classed under 'impressing others', leading to the terminal value 'status'. On the basis of the interviews with the students intending to continue their education, a means–end chain structure was compiled (see Figure 4.8).

continued . . .

This analysis led to the following, rather interesting, conclusions:

- The location of the university turned out to be very important to all respondents (because most of them did not intend to move out of their parental home). Universities are therefore competing on a local level, and not so much with other universities offering the same course in another city.
- Boys are more interested in how others view the course and the financial perspectives. Girls are led more by individual motives of interest and pleasure.

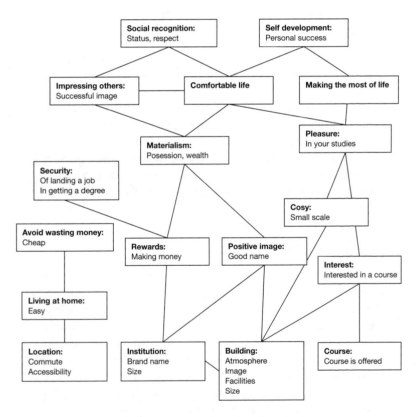

FIGURE 4.8 Means–end chain structure for university selection

4.3 Conclusions of target group analysis

In the final section of this chapter, we will draw some general conclusions regarding step 3 of the positioning analysis: target group analysis.

In Section 4.1 we detailed the structure of a (mental) brand schema. When positioning a brand, it is important to know what a brand schema essentially looks like (and how people store brand-related information in their brains). We described three mental connections:

1. The connection between brand and product class, for which we established that a brand has to differentiate itself from other brands in the same product class, while the brand manager should also bear in mind that the target group should indeed be able to classify the brand (i.e. the brand should not be differentiated too much, and consumers should still link it to a concrete product class). If consumers are unable to connect a brand to an existing category, the chances are that the brand will not survive.
2. The connection between brand and (associations with) attributes. On p. 82 we discussed two different types of attributes: product features and product benefits. Finally, we covered three aspects of the connection between the brand and attributes: contents, valency and strength of the connection.
3. The connection between the brand and values. The main conclusion here is that successful brands succeed in awarding meaning to attributes by linking them to values. On p. 85 we outlined three value levels (values relating to fundamental, social and personal needs).

Section 4.2 went on to explain a method (means–end analysis) that enables the linking of attributes to values, and furthermore made it clear how values can be deployed in the substantiation of concrete customer contacts. We first did this by focusing on target group selection, and subsequently on the output of a means–end analysis: means–end chains. On p. 92 we concluded by presenting methods for the compilation of means–end chains. This section ended with a concrete example of such a means–end analysis with four concrete steps.

This chapter has centred on the analysis of the target group, as part of the external analysis of the brand that is being positioned. The second step in this external analysis consists of charting the competition and assessing how competitors present themselves in the market. Chapter 5 will focus on this second step in the external analysis.

Notes

1. This estimate is based on a Dutch research project (Riezebos and Riezebos, 2004).
2. See, for example, Alba *et al.* (1991) and Krishnan (1996).
3. Farquhar and Herr (1993).
4. Batey (2008, pp. 4–5).
5. For a review of theory-based empirical research on categorization, see Loken (2006).
6. Brewer and Treyens (1981).
7. Sujan and Bettman (1989).
8. Source: Keller (2008, Chapter 3).
9. Loewy said the following about the MAYA principle: 'The adult public's taste is not necessarily ready to accept the logical solutions to their requirements if the solution implies too vast a departure from what they have been conditioned into accepting as the norm.' Source: www.raymondloewy.com/about/bio.html (accessed 28 December 2010).
10. Farquhar and Herr (1993); Keller (2008, pp. 528 and 544, note 71).
11. Music (such as an advertisement's signature tune) can also help call a brand name to mind.
12. Partly based on Keller *et al.* (2008, pp. 52–56).
13. Tybout *et al.* (1981).
14. Keller (2001).
15. Rokeach (1973).
16. NGO stands for non-governmental organization, an organization that has no ties to any government and that one way or another targets an assumed social interest. These are generally organizations working on promoting environmental causes, health causes, aid work or human rights (source: Wikipedia).
17. Gutman (1982); Reynolds and Gutman (1984, 2001).
18. Olson and Reynolds (1983).
19. Reynolds and Gutman (2001, p. 27).
20. Reynolds and Gutman (2001); see also Wansink (2003).
21. Reynolds and Gutman (1984).
22. As part of her final-year project for the Communication course at Inholland University, Margreet van Staalduijnen interviewed 12 secondary school students who were in the middle of selecting a university.

5
COMPETITOR ANALYSIS (STEP 4)

In Chapter 4 we analysed the target group for the brand we are positioning. This analysis is set in the sphere of the positioned brand's external environment. Another entity in that external target group is composed of the brand's competitors. In most markets the activities of competitors have consequences for the positioning options of a brand. In order to come to the right positioning, we therefore need to take stock of our competition and the positions claimed by our competitors. Figure 5.1 depicts the BTC model, with the competitors of the brand we are positioning in the bottom right circle.

In this chapter we will focus on two subjects: identifying competitors and assessing how these position themselves in the market. Section 5.1 first focuses

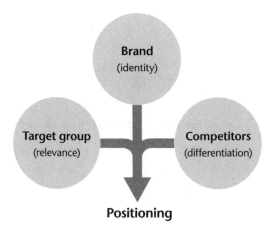

FIGURE 5.1 Competitors as part of the external analysis of a positioning process

on a model that can provide assistance when mapping the competition. Section 5.2 includes a description of no less than 14 possible approaches to positioning centred on the organization, the product, a marketing variable or the receiver. Section 5.3 concludes this chapter with examples of these positioning approaches for five different categories: fast-moving consumer goods, durable consumer goods, services, business-to-business and non-profit brands. This chapter is predominantly intended as a stepping stone when mapping the competition and their positioning choices.

5.1 Competition environment

In Table 4.2 (p. 88) we listed possible target groups for brand positioning. Dealing with the competitors issue also involves choosing a 'target group', namely those whom you will be considering your competitors. This choice depends on your market vision. In Section 2.5 we used the example of telecommunications providers and Internet providers, who, leading up to the millennium, would probably never have thought that their markets would converge in 10 years' time (the 'triple play' idea). At this point, it would be helpful to cast our mind back to the market vision and use the Five Forces Model (see Figure 5.2) to identify the competitors in the present market as best as possible, but also to identify any possible prospective new entrants that could play a role in your competition environment in the future. The Five Forces Model[1] distinguishes five sources of competition and places these in three main groups:

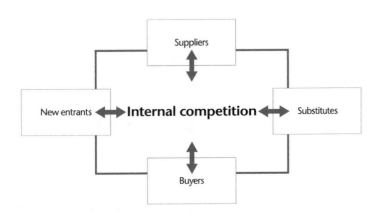

FIGURE 5.2 The Five Forces Model

- internal competition;
- external competition (suppliers and buyers);
- potential competition (new entrants and substitutes).

In the Five Forces Model *internal competition* refers to current competitors in a market. These competitors often seem obvious. However, when designating your competitors, it is key to beware of making the competition arena too small. When assessing the competition faced by Jaguar, you would naturally tend to consider Bentley, Mercedes and BMW as competitors. But it is less obvious to also consider that cheaper brands could also enter the prestige segment in which Jaguar operates. Toyota managed it with their luxury brand Lexus, Nissan followed suit by launching its own luxury brand Infiniti, and Volkswagen made an attempt with its Phaeton model. Any brand owner must always factor in that the competition environment is in a constant state of flux, and that a competitor that was initially believed to be an insignificant one can suddenly develop into one of the brand's most fearsome competitors. Not only can the internal competition environment change, but all kinds of external parties can also enter the internal competition environment. In the Five Forces Model these possible new entrants come from the group of external and potential competitors.

A brand's *external competitors* include buyers and suppliers. When suppliers enter the internal competition environment, we are dealing with forward, vertical integration. In the computer market, the microprocessor manufacturer Intel could decide to market its own brand of PCs. In the car market, Bosch, a supplier of many of the electronic components used in many brands' cars, could start assembling a car under its own brand name. Suppliers will generally only enter the internal competition environment when players from this environment themselves are turning to backward, vertical integration. That would, for example, be the case if Dell were to start developing processors and putting the Dell brand on them, hence driving Intel to start marketing Intel computers. Buyers can also intrude in the internal competition environment, as supermarkets do when their own brands start encroaching on the positions of renowned brands.

Apart from internal and external competition, a brand can also face *potential competition* (new entrants and substitutes). Taking the market of portable music players as an example of an internal competition environment, you could say that Apple can be considered a new entrant in this market. Sony had throughout the 1980s and the best part of the 1990s built a strong position as a manufacturer of portable music players. This position was so strong that the brand name that Sony used for this product category (Walkman) became the brandnomer, i.e. generic name, for personal stereo devices. At the start of this century, Apple intruded on this market of portable music players with the iPod, in combination with the iTunes application. Again, the brand (iPod) has virtually become the brandnomer for products in this category. Another form of potential competition is offered by substitutes. Skype (Internet telephony), for example, is a substitute for regular telephony. And PDFs can be regarded a substitute for the fax. In the latter case, this means that HP, a manufacturer of fax machines, should consider Adobe, maker of Acrobat software, as one of its competitors.

The merit of the Five Forces Model lies in the assistance it offers when mapping the competition – and then mainly by drawing attention to competitors that had initially been overlooked. However, this does not mean that a positioning process should always heed external and potential competitors. The idea is to come to a well-founded choice; after all, a positioning has to be able to last a minimum of three to four years. This makes it crucial that you be mindful of the fact that competition in a market is constantly subject to change.

After having identified all relevant competitors, you will have to figure out how these position themselves, because the idea is to differentiate your brand from the competitors' brands (see Figure 5.1). Since the 1970s, many research technologies have been developed to map competitor positionings on the basis of customer perceptions and evaluations. Multidimensional scaling (MDS) and discriminant analysis are the two principal techniques used to construct these cognitive maps.[2] We will now present a framework that helps to map competitor positionings on the basis of their respective positioning approaches towards customers. Section 5.2 describes 14 positioning categories, the so-called 'positioning approaches'. Section 5.3 further explains these categories for fast-moving consumer goods, durable consumer goods, services, business-to-business and non-profit brands.

5.2 Fourteen positioning approaches

Before you can choose a positioning for your brand, you will need to have a clear idea of how your competitors have positioned theirs. In order to map their brand positioning, we have identified 14 'positioning approaches' (or opportunities for differentiation) (see Table 5.1). A positioning approach is the choice of a central factor to base brand presentation on. For example, many products draw particular attention to product benefits or price. As brand

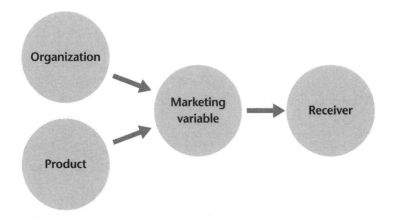

FIGURE 5.3 Four positioning approach categories

TABLE 5.1 Fourteen positioning approaches divided into four categories

Organization-based	Product-based	Marketing-variable-based	Receiver-based
Corporate ability	Prototypical	Price	Target group
Mentality	Product features	Distribution	Situation
Employee	Rational benefit	Design	Emotional benefit
		Name awareness	Value

communication will often stress several different aspects, it may be difficult to identify the starting point for the differentiation of the product in question. You may therefore struggle to place a brand in one of the 14 categories. The exercise of identifying positioning approaches is therefore intended as a way of gaining insight into how competitors present themselves in the market, rather than as a way of conducting a watertight analysis leading to exact and unambiguous pigeonholing of competitors.

Figure 5.3 presents the four categories of positioning approaches in diagrammatic form: approaches centred on the organization, the product, a marketing variable, or the receiver. Table 5.1 lists the relevant approaches per category.

Organization-based

When positioning a corporate brand – or a product brand – the main focus can be on corporate features. This principle can be split up into three practical positioning approaches: stressing the corporate abilities of the organization, stressing a certain mentality and placing the central focus on the employees.

When positioning on the basis of *corporate ability*, the emphasis is on the organization's core competencies. This involves a company (or institution) making it absolutely clear to its relevant target group that it, like no other company, has the ability to deliver specific goods and/or services. This approach is not used very commonly when positioning a brand. One example is Schiphol Airport Amsterdam, which draws attention to its ability to be much more than merely a place to catch your plane. Supported by the slogan 'Where else', Schiphol advertises the possibilities it offers travellers to relax, enjoy art, go shopping, have a delicious meal, and much more.

A brand can also be positioned in the market by emphasizing the organization's *mentality*: 'This is what we stand for' or 'That's how we do things here'. In such cases, the mentality in question is often initiated by the founder(s) of the company, such as at Virgin, founded by the rebel billionaire Richard Branson, and Ben & Jerry's.

There are also organizations that make their positioning revolve around their *employees*. In Chapter 2 we saw the example of Southwest Airlines, which puts its employees first in everything it undertakes. Crucial factors in the success of Southwest Airlines are, among other things, the leading role of the human resources management department and its articulation of the so-called 'Southwest Airlines Spirit' (which stems from friendliness, warmth and pride) and its dedication to 'positively outrageous service'. The success of such positioning depends largely on the actual behaviour displayed by employees.

Product-based

In many positioning strategies the product takes centre stage. That means the focus is on something the product (item or service) can do and/or provide. A product focus can engender three positioning approaches: prototypical or with product features or rational benefits as the basis for the positioning.

Prototypical positioning means that the brand claims to be the most typical representative of the product category. This claim is often made by brands that have acquired a very strong position in their market (such as TomTom) and/or whose name has become synonymous for the product category (such as iPod, Hoover and Kleenex). TomTom, for example, claims to provide all the benefits that matter in the car navigation systems category: easy-to-use, smart and complete (see Box 5.1). Prototypical positioning is often confused with corporate ability-based positioning. But prototypical positioning always revolves around the product, whereas corporate ability highlights the organization. Not that this removes all confusion – because what if the organization itself is the product (as in the case of retailers)? Later in this chapter, under services including retailing, we have chosen to consider such cases as prototypical positioning.

Snack-a-Jacks rice cakes contain less than 5 per cent fat. That is the *product feature* that is highlighted in Snack-a-Jacks advertising. This is a kind of positioning that is often used by food products. Technological products also often push certain product features in their positioning, such as: 'Potential 3000 Watt', '10 million megapixels and 10× optical zoom' and 'Hybrid drive mechanism'. Services also have product features that can be underlined in advertising, such as opening hours (7-Eleven), availability ('24-hour availability'), waiting times ('Ready while you wait') and response times ('A reply within 2 days').

Positioning based on a *rational benefit* sees a provider claim a benefit that is generated by a product feature. But that product feature does not necessarily have to be mentioned.[4] Sensodyne communication, for example, always states that this brand of toothpaste protects sensitive teeth, but does not mention which product features provide that protection.

BOX 5.1 TOMTOM[3]

'TomTom Go is the world's easiest-to-use, smartest and most complete car navigation solution.

Easy Click Magnetic mount
Latest map guarantee
Local Search with Google™
Spoken street names
Richer maps
Map Share™ technology
Advanced lane guidance
Rich Points of Interest'

Marketing-variable-based

As well as centring a positioning on the organization or the product, positioning can also be based on a marketing variable. We have split this category up into four positioning approaches that each focus on one specific marketing variable: positioning on the basis of price, distribution, design or name awareness.

A positioning approach based on *price* makes the selling price the product's main puller, offsetting it against differently priced products. Price-based positioning does not, however, mean that the brand in question always sells at the lowest price. Europe's largest retailer of home electronics, Media Markt, has, for example, been criticized on various occasions for not actually being the cheapest consumer electronics retailer out there – which it does claim to be. Price-based positioning can be organized in different ways:

- 'The same for less': this strategy is often used to provide a positive offset against a larger market party (mostly the market leader). The challenger brand then offers more or less the same product at a lower price, as supermarket own brands do, as well as Škoda with its 'Simply Clever' campaign.
- 'Less for less': this strategy is used by relatively major players; they cut frills to be able to charge less (no-frills airlines, such as EasyJet and Ryanair, do this: flights are cheaper because there is no free food and drink on board).
- 'Can't get it cheaper elsewhere': the emphasis here is on offering the absolutely lowest price, enabled by sweeping cost containment (e.g. Aldi and Lidl).

Distribution-based positioning can accentuate a number of different distribution-related aspects. A brand can be differentiated using the claim that it is available only from specialist stores. Royal Canin pet-food products, for example, are only available from specialized retailers. Another form of distribution-based positioning sees brands claiming to have shortened the distribution column (by removing a link from the chain). One example was Dell computers, which up to 2007 only sold its products online.

In the case of *design*-based positioning, the appearance of the product or its packaging is the main feature that is stressed to differentiate the brand in the market. Well-known examples are Apple, Dyson and Bang & Olufsen. Brands using this positioning tactic either use design for aesthetic reasons (i.e. the product just looks good, such as Absolut Vodka bottles) or to draw

Competitor analysis (Step 4)

attention to product or packaging functionality (such as Dyson, where the transparent design serves to emphasize the revolutionary functioning of the cleaner).

Some brands base their positioning on *name awareness*. Their main aim is then to increase or uphold levels of brand name awareness. A commonly known example is the city and state of New York's slogan 'I love NY'. The only thing a consumer is intended to remember from this kind of communication is the brand name. Such communication will generally add little value to the brand.

Receiver-based

The last pending positioning approach category is the one that revolves around the receiver. This approach comes in four different forms: stressing a stereotypical target group, claiming a situation, drawing attention to an emotional benefit and claiming a value.

When positioning claims a *target group*, the brand in question attempts to appeal to a certain (stereotypical) target group on the basis of reasons that

bear no relation to the actual product. Bacardi, for one, tries to claim the target group of clubbing youngsters through music (B-Live).

An approach for successful positioning can also stem from claiming a *situation*. A very well-known example of this is After Eight, Nestlé's after-dinner mint. Another chocolaty example is Merci, a brand of chocolates that positions itself as the best small gift to give someone by way of saying thank you for something, which is also reflected in the name. And we should not overlook the confectionary brand Kit Kat here, with its slogan 'Have a break, have a Kit Kat'.

A clear example of positioning based on an *emotional benefit* is Axe deodorant, which bears the name Lynx in the UK. Axe offers a range of personal care products with seductive fragrances for young men. It positions itself as any young man's best weapon in the struggle to impress the opposite sex. The benefit offered is 'The Axe Effect', which makes Axe users irresistible to women. Axe promises an emotional benefit in a social context (vis-à-vis the opposite sex). L'Oréal also claims an emotional benefit, but not in a social context ('L'Oréal; because I'm worth it').

Value-based positioning seeks to tie into the target group's deeper motivations. This can be their need for safety and security, happiness, friendship, or status. The emphasis is on the symbolic meaning the brand adds to a product (goods or services). One brand claiming a reasonably fundamental value is Volvo ('safety'). Nokia is a good example of a brand targeting relational values in terms of Maslow's hierarchy of needs ('Connecting people').

The abovementioned 14 positioning approaches come together in a handy checklist that can be used to map the competition. But we should reiterate that brands do not necessarily limit themselves to one approach. The computer manufacturer Dell, for example, claimed for several years that their computers were cheaper precisely because they had cut out the middleman. This was dual positioning based on price and distribution.

At this stage of the external positioning analysis, it may prove quite tricky to identify competitors for each of the listed positioning approaches. We have therefore included examples of five different product groups in Section 5.3.

5.3 Market exploration in terms of positionings

In this section we will review the positioning approaches again for each of the brand categories: fast-moving consumer goods (FMCGs), durable consumer goods, services, business-to-business and non-profit brands. We will introduce each brand category by way of a brief description. And we will subsequently provide examples of each positioning approach within that brand category. These examples may not always be traced back to reality in the same way as we describe them, but they do represent the general directions that match the brand in question.

Fast-moving consumer goods

FMCGs comprise a broad scale of widely sold, fast-moving consumer products, such as food, drinks, toiletries (including soap and cosmetics), cleaning products, detergents and other non-durable products (glasses, light bulbs, batteries and plastic disposables for household use). Well-known providers of such products include multinationals such as Nestlé, Unilever and Procter & Gamble, as well as companies such as Sara Lee, with a wide range of products in this category, and the Bolton Group. Table 5.2 lists examples of the different positioning approaches for FMCGs.

An example of the organization-based positioning approach with a focus on corporate ability is Cuprinol, the brand leader in the garden woodcare sector. Cuprinol claims to be the most competent in the woodcare market via year-on-year leadership in innovation. One brand that bases its positioning on a corporate mentality is Ben & Jerry's. In their own words, 'a company has a responsibility towards the community in which it operates'. Despite this serious undertone, Ben & Jerry's is still a fun brand. This is apparent not only from their advertising – it is also something they put in the names of the ice cream flavours they market (such as Socialice, Peace of Cake and Cherry Garcia, after Jerry Garcia, the late Grateful Dead singer). Hertog Jan beer, a traditional Dutch beer from the portfolio of Inbev, has been placing its central focus on its employees for a while now; the brand tries to stand out by portraying its employees showing exquisite craftsmanship and a drive for perfection (further reinforced by the playing of Fairground Attraction's hit 'It's Got to be Perfect' in their TV ads).

Under *product-based* positioning, Heineken serves as a classic example of prototypical positioning. In the 1990s, the brand ran several campaigns that equated ordering a beer to ordering a Heineken. Their 'Serving the Planet' campaign further continued this brand's prototypical approach. Alfa Bier, on the other hand, a beer brewed by an independent family-owned brewery established in 1870, is a brand that highlights product features by pointing out that it is the only brewery in the Netherlands to extract its brewing water from a spring certified by the Dutch Ministry of Health, Welfare and Sport

TABLE 5.2 Examples of positioning approaches for FMCGs

Positioning approach	Brand	Note
Organization-based		
Corporate ability	Cuprinol	'No one knows garden wood care like we do'
Mentality	Ben & Jerry's	Claiming corporate social responsibility and 'fun'
Employee	Hertog Jan beer	Brewers striving for perfection (use of Fairground Attraction's classic 'It's Got to be Perfect' in TV ad)
Product-based		
Prototypical	Heineken	'Serving the Planet'
Product features	Alfa beer	Beer brewed using spring water
	Flora margarine	'80% less saturated fat than butter'
Rational benefit	Vanish, Cillit Bang	Stain removal
Marketing-variable-based		
Price	Euro Shopper	Cheap assortment of supermarket products
Distribution	Vichy skincare products	Only available from pharmacies
Design	Absolut Vodka	Bottle design
Name awareness	Heinz Baked Beans	'Beanz Meanz Heinz'
Receiver-based		
Target group	Bacardi	B-Live
Situation	Kit Kat	'Have a break, have a Kit Kat'
Emotional benefit	L'Oréal	'Because I'm worth it'
Value	Werther's Original	Family tradition

(22 March 1995).[5] Alfa's tagline is therefore not simply 'beer', but rather 'Edel Pils' (Sublime Pilsner). Another good example of positioning on a feature is Unilever's Flora margarine, which claims to have 80 per cent less saturated fat than butter. The cleaning products Vanish and Cillit Bang are good examples of brands claiming a rational benefit. Their Websites list the following claims, among others:

- 'Vanish removes even the most stubborn stains in clothes, carpets and curtains. Vanish Oxi Action is suitable for both coloured and white fabrics.'
- 'Thanks to the revolutionary, power cleaner formula, Cillit Bang will remove even the toughest stains and stubborn dirt in seconds – every day, anywhere in the house!'

The story goes that the latter product was initially called Cillit, and that the word 'Bang' was added to stress the cleaning power of the product.

Examples of FMCG brands whose positioning is based on a *marketing variable* include the following:

- Price: Euro Shopper is a brand of supermarket products owned by AMS Sourcing and is sold in various supermarket chains in Iceland, Ireland, Norway, Sweden, Finland, the Baltic states, the Netherlands, Portugal and Greece.
- Distribution: Vichy skincare products (dermatologically tested and allergy-tested cosmetics and personal care products) are only available from authorized pharmacies.
- Design: Absolut Vodka is a prime example of a brand whose advertising has laid a clear emphasis on the aesthetic appeal of its bottle.
- Name awareness: the well-known slogan 'Beanz Meanz Heinz' is mainly targeted at upholding Heinz brand name awareness in the baked-beans segment.

Finally, you can also distinguish FMCG positionings where the *receiver* is the main target. We mentioned Bacardi earlier, with its positioning that seeks to pull in a specific target group (clubbing youngsters) through music (B-Live). The chocolate bar Kit Kat intends to be the ideal hunger-busting snack. L'Oréal, on the other hand, features an emotional benefit for consumers: women, and men too, should permit themselves the luxury of these products because they are worth it. Werther's Original is an example that has been highlighting family values that are relevant to the receiver for years. In the TV commercials for this brand of sweets, a kind-hearted grandfather bonds together with his grandson, thereby stressing the importance of family tradition.

Durable consumer goods

Durable consumer goods are goods intended for long-term, and therefore repeated, use. Maintenance and/or repairs can ensure that these goods last for a very long time. The most widely used criterion for being a durable consumer good is that it has to have a lifespan of at least three years. Examples of durable consumer goods are cars, electronic devices, furniture, toys, tools and kitchen appliances. In contrast to FMCGs, these products are generally sold by specialist retailers (such as car dealerships, furniture stores, clothes shops, toy shops, white goods retailers, and the like). This is down to the fact that people need specific advice when purchasing durable consumer goods. Table 5.3 lists examples of various positioning approaches for durable consumer goods.

An example of *organization-based* positioning with a corporate ability focus used for durables is BMW's Efficient Dynamics campaign, which it launched in 2008. This campaign stresses BMW's ability to push back fuel consumption through a range of innovations (such as brake-energy regeneration) without compromising on driving performance. GSUS (clothing brand), on the other hand, is a brand that places the emphasis on its mentality through its motto 'Welcome to heaven's playground'. This refers to this brand's first store ('Heaven's Playground'), whose founders went by the motto 'Do what you like best and design what you would like to wear.' An example of a durable consumer item manufacturer that focuses its marketing on its employees is Gibson guitars. In reference to the production of the Gibson Vintage Original Spec, they even go so far as to claim that 'the brilliant guitar builders of the Custom Shop have (re)produced these historic guitars with a solid body with utmost precision'. In this kind of positioning of durables, communication will generally place the emphasis on craftsmanship.

An example of prototypical *product-based* positioning is provided by the durables producer Volkswagen. Early in 2008, it came up with the pay-off 'Volkswagen. Das Auto' for the global market. Miele is another example of a brand claiming a prototypical positioning through its pay-offs 'Always better' in the UK and 'Immer besser' in Germany and France. Geox is a brand that mainly positions itself on the basis of a single product feature. All their shoes and clothing 'breathe'. The focus is on their patented breathing system that leads to a new sense of well-being. JVC, on the other hand, is a brand that uses its slogan 'The Perfect Experience' to highlight product benefits for

TABLE 5.3 Examples of positioning approaches for durable consumer goods

Positioning approaches	Brand	Note
Organization-based		
Corporate ability	BMW Efficient Dynamics	BMW manages to make sure that its commitment to the environment is not at the expense of the ultimate driving experience
Mentality	GSUS	'Welcome to heaven's playground'
Employee	Gibson	'Brilliant Guitar Builders'
Product-based		
Prototypical	Volkswagen	'Volkswagen. Das Auto'
	Miele	'Always Better' (UK), 'Immer besser' (Germany, France)
Product features	Geox	The 'Geox breathes patented system'
Rational benefit	JVC	'The Perfect Experience'
Marketing-variable-based		
Price	Dacia	'Think big, pay little'
Distribution	Dell	Formerly only available to consumers and companies directly from Dell's website (no middlemen)
Design	Alessi	Italian design
Name awareness	Mazda	'Zoom, zoom, zoom'
Receiver-based		
Target group	O'Neill	Surfers
Situation	Senseo	'Good coffee, any time of day'
Emotional benefit	Diesel	'Diesel, for successful living'
Value	Microsoft	'Realize your potential'

consumers. Their video projector advertising, for example, not only extols their contrast capacities and powerful video processing virtues (product features), but also presents a projector that provides a breathtakingly clear picture and creates a true cinema feeling (i.e. product benefits).

Examples of durables brands whose positioning is based on a *marketing variable* include the following:

- Price: Dacia is a Renault subsidiary that positions itself with the slogan 'Think big, pay little'.
- Distribution: Dell computers only used to sell its products online up to 2007.
- Design: Alessi is an Italian brand marketing designer kitchen appliances.
- Name awareness: the carmaker Mazda uses a catchy song in its TV ads, entitled 'zoom, zoom, zoom'; these ads provide very little substantial arguments for buying a Mazda.

In the *receiver-based* group, the surfing brand O'Neill relentlessly tries to claim the target group that naturally goes with the brand (surfers). The Senseo coffee maker promises a fresh cup of coffee at any time of day (situation). Diesel targets (with a healthy dose of irony) an emotional benefit with its pay-off 'Diesel, for successful living' and, finally, Microsoft emphasizes a value by claiming that its software contributes to the realization of your potential ('Realize your potential').

Services (including retail)

A service is a product with largely immaterial specifics, such as a haircut, booking a holiday, having a public notary make your will or hiring a car. Services differ from consumer goods in three ways: services have an immaterial, or intangible, component; they are transitory because production and consumption happen at the same time (you cannot store a service for future consumption); and a service is a form of interactive consumption, with the buyer being part of the delivered 'product'. Although a service is of an immaterial nature, it can also be provided in combination with a product, such as the pizza delivery service offered by a pizza restaurant. The material/immaterial ratio can vary. A pop concert is, apart from the food and beverages consumed at the event, not a physical product; a mortgage is only a physical product to a limited degree (the actual policy sheet); and a pizza delivery service is complementary to a physical product (in the case of the latter, the service – home delivery of the pizza – could indeed lead consumers to specifically buy from the pizzeria providing that service).

Retailing is a separate form of service provision. 'Retail' entails the provision of services and/or goods to consumers for personal use. These can be physical products (such as at a supermarket), but also immaterial products, such as holidays and insurance policies. The term 'retail' is also used by service providers to denote the business unit that is responsible for customer contacts but does not have its own physical outlets. Table 5.4 lists examples of various positioning approaches for services, including retailing.

An example of an *organization-based* positioning approach highlighting a service provider's corporate ability is TNT mail services, which uses the tagline 'Sure we can'. A fine example of a service placing the central focus on the organization's mentality is Virgin, which is always on the lookout for markets where it can startle sleeping giants with its unorthodox methods. Services often assume an employee-based approach; this is something that not only the major consultancy firms do – retail companies are not averse to this tactic either. One example is Zappos.com, founded in 1999 with the objective of becoming the prime destination for online shoe shopping. Their unwavering focus on superior customer service has allowed them to expand online offerings to include handbags, clothing, electronics and much more. The focus on service is effectuated through an even stronger focus on the employee experience. In an interview Tony Hsieh, CEO of Zapppos.com, stresses the importance of the Zappos.com culture for delivering the best customer service (see Box 5.2).

Examples of services with a *product-based* positioning approach are WeightWatchers, which has been successfully claiming a leading position in the slimming market for over 40 years, and Harrods, the mother of all luxury department stores. Their positionings can be considered prototypical ones. TripAdvisor, an online reviewing platform for and by travellers, differentiates itself on the basis of the product feature claim 'Over 20 million traveller reviews and opinions'. Ibis, part of the Accor group, has 769 hotels worldwide that deliver the rational benefit 'round-the-clock service at budget prices'. Yousendit.com positions itself by using the rational benefit of offering the possibility of sending large files over the Internet.

In the service sector there are also a range of examples of *marketing-variable-based* positioning:

- Price: the budget airline Ryanair and budget hotel chain Formule 1 (also part of the Accor group) are clear price fighters focusing on a minimum

TABLE 5.4 Examples of positioning approaches for services (including retailing)

Positioning approaches	Brand	Note
Organization-based		
Corporate ability	TNT	'Sure we can'
Mentality	Virgin	Rebellious
Employee	Zappos.com	'Powered by service'
Product-based		
Prototypical	WeightWatchers	'Over 40 years of experience in weight loss'
	Harrods	'The world's most famous luxury department store'
Product features	TripAdvisor	'Over 20 million traveller reviews and opinions'
Rational benefit	Ibis Hotels	'Round-the-clock service at budget prices'
	Yousendit.com	'Send large files'
Marketing-variable-based		
Price	Ryanair	'Cheap flights'
	Formule 1 Hotels	'Pay less, travel more'
Distribution	Tesco Delivery Service	'Delivered to your door 7 days a week'
Design	Google	Simple, easy-to-use 'search engine'
Name awareness	US Airways	'Fly with US'
Receiver-based		
Target group	Pullman	'High-end establishments dedicated to the business traveller'
Situation	I4gotyourbirthday.co.uk	Send a card the same day
Emotional benefit	Sofitel	'French art de vivre'
	Club Med	'Where happiness means the world'
Value	Hallmark e-cards	'Communicating love and friendship'

BOX 5.2 THE ZAPPOS.COM CULTURE[6]

'I think most businesses probably just don't care about customer service period. But then, even for the ones that do, they go about it in a very process-and-procedure way. And basically it comes down to basically developing a series of scripts, which is okay, but it's like talking to a machine.

'Our approach is no scripts and not to measure efficiency in terms of the call times, which is how most call centers are run. Instead, we focus on the culture and make sure everyone in the company understands our long-term vision about building a Zappos brand to be about the very best customer service. We make sure to give them the proper training to use all the tools and so on. But then leave it up to them to just be real and genuine and passionate when they're actually talking to customers.

'Everyone hired goes through the same training that our call center reps go through. It is four weeks long, and we go over company history, our philosophy about customer service and points of company culture. And then they are actually on the phone for two weeks taking calls from customers. After that you start the job that you're actually hired to do. During that training process, at the end of the first week, we make an offer. The offer is that we'll pay you $2,000 to leave the company. And that's a standing offer until the end of the training. The reason for that is because we don't want people who are here just for a paycheck.'

of extras and maximum cost efficiency in order to be able to offer their customers the lowest possible prices.
- Distribution: Tesco's Delivery Service's promise to deliver groceries 'to your door 7 days a week' is testimony to Tesco's confidence in its distribution expertise.
- Design: more than any other service provider, Google cottoned on to the fact that searching for information online should be all about the search query. Its plain and easy-to-use design has helped Google differentiate itself from other search engines. The emphasis is on functional differentiation through design.

- Name awareness: this positioning approach is all about firmly planting the brand name in the target group's mind. 'Fly with US' is intended to equate the pronoun 'us' with US Airways to basically make the target group part of the brand name, and ultimately maximize brand awareness.

Finally, there is the *receiver-based* approach, which can also be applied to position services. After Ibis and Formule 1, we will now draw on two other examples from the Accor group: Pullman and Sofitel. While Ibis and Formule 1 are positioned on a rational benefit and price respectively, Pullman targets a specific market segment, namely business travellers. Accor's other high-end hotel chain, Sofitel, adds an emotional benefit to that, namely 'French art de vivre'. If you ever find yourself in the situation where you have forgotten to send a loved one a birthday card, you can turn to I4gotyourbirthday.co.uk. This British-based Website enables you to send an actual paper birthday card that same day. Hallmark is another player in the birthday cards market. In the e-cards segment, Hallmark positions itself strongly on the values of love and friendship, which it also does in the market for paper cards.

Business-to-business

Business-to-business companies (b-to-b, B2B companies) supply products and/or services to other companies and not directly to consumers. B-to-b companies differ from business-to-consumer companies (b-to-c) in a number of ways. B-to-b companies often have fewer customers and greater sales volumes per customer than b-to-c companies. And b-to-b companies often also employ well-trained buyers with excellent negotiation skills, which they deploy in purchase price negotiations. Buying decisions of b-to-b companies are mostly made by buyer teams, and are based on rational arguments. This does not, however, mean that emotional arguments never feature in b-to-b markets; emotions do play a role here, although purchase decisions in b-to-b markets always have to be able to be justified by rational arguments. Another key difference between b-to-b and b-to-c markets is that the former category tends to have longer-lasting relations between buyers and sellers. That is partly down to the fact that the selling party pursues intensive customer relationship management (CRM) as well as the fact that switching suppliers is often far too expensive to hop from one supplier to the next. Table 5.5 lists various examples of positioning approaches for b-to-b companies.

TABLE 5.5 Examples of positioning approaches for b-to-b companies

Positioning approaches	Brand	Note
Organization-based		
Corporate ability	Impress	'Metal packaging solutions'
Mentality	DSM	'Unlimited. DSM'
Employee	PriceWaterhouse Coopers	'Connected Thinking'
Product-based		
Prototypical	McKinsey & Company	'The Firm'
Product features	DAF trucks	'Build to order'
Rational benefit	Nestlé Waters Direct	All-in-one solution for water coolers
Marketing-variable-based		
Price	Google Apps	Google innovation. Powerful solutions. Low cost.
Distribution	FedEx	'The World on Time'
Design	Vitra	Developing furniture in collaboration with cutting-edge designers
Name awareness	Double A paper	'Double A paper, double quality paper'
Receiver-based		
Target group	Océ	'Printing for Professionals'
Situation	Office Christmas	'Make your office Christmas party the best yet'
Emotional benefit	Philips Healthcare	'Healthcare without boundaries'
Value	Bosch	'Technology for life'

For an example of *organization-based* positioning with a corporate ability focus in a b-to-b company, we have turned to Impress, a leading metal packaging group resulting from the merger of the metal packaging interests of Pechiney (France) and Schmalbach-Lubeca (Germany). Brand positioning is based on this young group's corporate ability in the area of metal packaging solutions, honed throughout the history of the various constituent parts. The life sciences and materials sciences giant DSM, on the other hand, intends to let us know through its slogan 'Unlimited. DSM' that their organization is imbued with pioneering spirit. DSM hence emphasizes a mentality in its positioning. PricewaterhouseCoopers (PwC), one of the Big Four international accountancy firms, chose in 2003 to place the central focus on its employees using the slogan 'Connected Thinking'. This positioning pointed to 'the organization's strength as a sophisticated global network of experienced individuals that share ideas, methodologies and expertise to solve client problems'[7] (see Box 5.3).

For *product-based* positioning, McKinsey & Company is an example of a company that has carved out a prototypical position for itself in the market. Even though this company is currently presenting itself with the pay-off 'challenge your ambition', it has built a position as the strategy consulting standard in the past few decades. This is best expressed in the company's nickname: 'The Firm'. DAF Trucks, a subsidiary of the North American corporation PACCAR, is a company that stresses product features. This truck

---

BOX 5.3 PRICEWATERHOUSECOOPERS (PWC): 'CONNECTED THINKING'[8]

'Where do great ideas come from? More often than not, they start with the ability to take what's been learned in one discipline and apply it to another. We call this ability Connected Thinking. Connected Thinking is about stretching ourselves to bring new perspectives that challenge conventional thoughts and solutions. It's about working together and drawing on our collective knowledge to bring world-class thinking to our clients, and to benefit all parts of their organization. It means being anti-silo. It means crossing traditional boundaries, staying truly multi-disciplinary, and actively seeking out different perspectives to unlock a fresh answer to a problem. Connected Thinking is PricewaterhouseCoopers' way to better solutions.'

manufacturer works according to the 'Build to Order' principle, meaning that all vehicles are built to satisfy each customer's individual wishes regarding product features. A b-to-b company with a positioning focus on a rational benefit is Nestlé Waters Direct, which delivers water coolers to offices. The benefit claimed is that it provides the best all-in-one solution by offering several models of water coolers, their Aquarel brand water, accessories, and convenient delivery, installation and service.

We found the following examples of *marketing variable-based* positioning in the b-to-b sector:

- Price: Google Apps offers organizations email hosting, information sharing, agenda management and more services at very low cost.
- Distribution: FedEx's deep-rooted passion for on-time delivery leads them to organize themselves in such a way that these distribution skills lead to the fulfilment of their promise 'The World on Time'.
- Design: Vitra, established in 1950, has been manufacturing furniture designed by Charles and Ray Eames and George Nelson since 1957. These were the origins of a company that today differentiates itself as the developer of furniture in collaboration with modern designers.
- Name awareness: in the market for copying and printing paper, Double A paper established itself through its striking communication, which was fully geared towards implanting the brand name in people's brains. This company has meanwhile moved on to highlighting the superior quality of its paper.

Océ, a b-to-b company whose history we discussed at length in Chapter 1, positions itself using the slogan 'Printing for Professionals'. That puts the onus onto the receiver, and the target group in particular. Office Christmas offers the best and hassle free office Christmas parties via their website officechristmas.co.uk. With this they set out to claim the event of organizing office Christmas parties, which is an example of a specific situation. Philips Healthcare has set its sights on hospitals and clinics through a proposition that can be characterized as an emotional benefit: 'Healthcare without boundaries'. Finally, Bosch sets out a market position by claiming a value: 'Technology for life'.

Non-profit

Non-profit covers a wide spectrum of organizations and activities that do not seek to realize profits. The objective of a non-profit organization is to support private or public affairs for non-commercial social ends. These ends can lie in a wide variety of realms, ranging from the arts and education to politics, research or aid work. Non-profit organizations come in two shapes: those that do not make money and are given a budget by a third party to fund their activities (mainly government institutions, such as any country's tax administration and competition commission), and those that do make a profit, but never explicitly set out to do so (this category is often referred to as *not-for-profit* organizations). In the latter category we mainly find charities, such as Amnesty International and Greenpeace. Table 5.6 lists examples of various positioning approaches for non-profit organization (including not-for-profit).

An example of *organization-based* positioning with a corporate ability focus on non-profit companies is Dubai, which tries to position itself as an economic hub between the West and the East. Their ability to be an economic hub probably needs to be stressed because Dubai is predominantly associated as a destination for a luxurious vacation. The German federal state of North Rhine–Westphalia provides a fine example of a non-profit organization positioning itself on the basis of a mentality claim. Their claim is one of open-mindedness and innovative spirit in their people, and intends to incite organizations to choose this region for expansion of their business. A campaign revolving around (potential) employees is one by the British Army. Their longstanding reputation for professionalism and being the best is articulated in their 'Join the professionals' slogan, placing the army's utterly professional staff at the heart of the positioning.

For *product-based* positioning we can turn to the Vincent van Gogh Museum for an example, because this world famous museum is a non-profit organization that uses its uniqueness in its prototypical positioning. The museum claims to have the largest collection of Vincent van Gogh paintings, and has even captured this product feature in its name. It also has works by Courbet, Gauguin, Jongkind and Monet in its collection, but that is not reflected in the museum's name. The One Percent Foundation asks its donors to structurally donate 1 per cent of their income for charity purposes. Not more and not less. Even including the name, this is a nice example of positioning on a feature. The city of Hong Kong clearly positions itself on the basis of the rational benefit of its unique blend of Eastern and Western influences.

In the *marketing-variable-based* positioning cluster we have found the following examples to illustrate these positioning tactics:

TABLE 5.6 Examples of positioning approaches for non-profit organisations

Positioning approaches	Brand	Note
Organization-based		
Corporate ability	Dubai	'The leading economic hub'
Mentality	North Rhine–Westphalia	'We love the new'
Employee	British Army	'Join the professionals'
Product-based		
Prototypical	Van Gogh Museum	The largest collection of paintings by Vincent van Gogh in the world.
Product features	One Percent Foundation	Donate 1% of your income for charity purposes
Rational benefit	Hong Kong	A dynamic metropolis steeped in unique blends of East and West
Marketing-variable-based		
Price	London Pass	'Visit over 55 attractions for one price!'
Distribution	DirectGov (UK government's online portal)	'Public services all in one place'
Design	Bilbao	Modern
Name awareness	New York	'I love NY'
Receiver-based		
Target group	Mama Cash	International women's fund. By and for women
Situation	Edinburgh	Ideal city break, 'Inspiring capital', well-known festival city
Emotional benefit	HM Revenue and Customs (UK Tax department)	'Tax doesn't have to be taxing'
Value	Amnesty International	'Support our fight for human rights'

- Price: the London Pass's price-based positioning promises substantial savings with the slogan 'Visit over 55 attractions for one price!' The success of the London Pass has led the company behind the London Pass, The Leisure Pass Group, to also introduce such passes for Paris and Berlin. Other cities have seen similar initiatives (below).
- Distribution: Directgov is the official UK government website for citizens, which makes a range of public services available all in one place, with an eye to boosting distribution and uptake of public services.
- Design: Bilbao presents itself as a modern city with the Guggenheim Museum for modern art by the architect Frank O. Gehry and several subway stations designed by Norman Foster.
- Name awareness: in the case of the city of New York (I love NY)[9] the emphasis is not so much on anything relating specifically to the city, but rather on the communication itself. The catchiness and cleverness of the slogan is what sticks in people's brains.

To wrap up this section on non-profit organization positioning, we will now focus on several that place the emphasis on the *receiver*. Mama

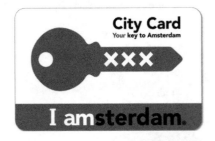

Cash is a charity that places its target group centre stage; it is an international women's fund run by women. It invests in small-scale, innovative projects with an eye to realizing a just and better future for women and girls. The Scottish capital Edinburgh, on the other hand, is capitalizing on a situation it is often associated with. It reinforces its city break destination appeal with the slogan 'Ideal city break', claiming it is an ideal place for a short vacation in an inspiring city. An example of a non-profit organization targeting an emotional benefit is the British tax department, HM Revenue and Customs, with its pay-off 'Tax doesn't have to be taxing', promising to make filing tax returns and other tax procedures less complicated. An example of value-centred positioning in the non-profit sector is provided by Amnesty International. This organization has been dedicating its efforts to seeing to compliance with the Universal Declaration of Human Rights since 1961, attempting to get people on its side by appealing to their values using the slogan 'Support our fight for human rights'. The Universal Declaration of Human Rights includes 30 articles, such as freedom, self-determination and dignity. The emotional benefit on offer is that you would be helping to safeguard human rights by supporting Amnesty International.

In closing

We have now come to the end of four chapters on brand positioning analysis. We first covered the internal part of the analysis, focusing on corporate identity and brand architecture (Chapters 2 and 3 respectively). This was followed by discussion of external positioning analysis, covering both the target group and the competition (Chapters 4 and 5 respectively). After these analyses, the time has now come to start making some serious choices for our brand's positioning. Chapter 6 will deal with these choices, and provide guidelines for the completion of a 'Brand Positioning Sheet'. But first up is Checklist 2, which will help you record the main conclusions from the external analysis.

Notes

1 Porter (1998, Chapter 1).
2 Green *et al.* (1989); Myers (1996, pp. 181–182); Hooley *et al.* (2008).
3 Source: www.tomtom.com (accessed 29 December 2010).
4 Carpenter *et al.* (1994).
5 Source: www.alfa-bier.nl (accessed 29 December 2010).

6 From Internet article/interview: 'Not your ordinary shoe salesman: how corporate culture sells more than a billion dollars of shoes a year', by Nick Nanton. Source: www.under30ceo.com (accessed 30 December 2010).
7 Source: www.wolffolins.com (accessed 30 December 2010).
8 Source: www.clubs.psu.edu/up/pwc/cthinking (accessed 30 December 2010).
9 The pay-off 'I love NY' relates to both the city and the state of New York.

CHECKLIST 2

Summary of the external analysis

In Chapters 4 and 5 we covered the external analysis as part of the positioning process. In the following we will summarize the main steps from this analysis. This allows you to go through the information about target groups and competitors again. The order in which subjects are presented here differs from the sequence used in Chapters 4 and 5. This is down to the fact that the means–end analyses usually already include names of competitors.

The brand's playing field

1. Identify the target group(s) the new positioning will focus on.
2. Set the (product) category the brand can be classed in, as seen from the point of view of the selected target group.
3. Use the Five Forces Model to identify internal, external and potential competitors.

Optional questions

In order to gain initial insight into the brand's mental environment, you can answer the following questions. Answering these questions is not strictly necessary for brand positioning, but it will give you a clear idea of how people view your brand.

1. What attributes do people generally associate with the product class the brand falls into, what attributes do they associate with the brand in question and what attributes do they associate with competing brands? Note that what you are basically asked to do here is to identify POPs ('points of parity') and PODs ('points of difference').

2   With regard to associations with attributions for their own brand, apart from describing the associations, also state what their valency is (positive or negative) and how strongly the associations are linked to the brand.
3   Try to assess the values that are associated with a brand. This is only possible through a means–end analysis, but the answers to the previous two questions could already help you to a sufficient extent in the assessment of the level of the values (fundamental, social or personal need) (see p. 85) and which actual values that could entail.

Means–end analysis

Approach a group of about ten people from the target group and ask them if they would mind being interviewed (duration about one hour per interview).[1] Start off by asking who they are and how they relate to the product class in question. Do not limit the interview to one or two contact domains (if the brand in question is a retailer, do not only focus on shop design and advertising used by this retailer). Then go on to figure out the means–end chains for a respondent using the methods described on p. 92. You can use

---

CHECKLIST FORM 2.1

Individual means–end chain for market/brand   _____

Respondent: _____

Domain/customer contact moment: _____

* * *

Terminal value(s)   _____

Instrumental value(s)   _____

Psycho-social meaning(s)   _____

Functional meaning(s)   _____

Benefit(s)   _____

Feature(s)   _____

Checklist Form 2.1 to record a respondent's means–end chain; do bear in mind that there is no need to always complete all six levels. Although we have only provided one column, working on the assumption that you will only reveal one value for a respondent, there can quite conceivably be several values at play. You can do these exercises for the market/product class as a whole, but you should at least do this for the brand in question.

During the interview you may come up against two problems:[2]

1. A respondent does not know why he considers something important. You can in that case use one of two techniques to dig up the required information:

    a) Ask the respondent what would happen if a certain attribute or benefit were to disappear.
    b) Place the subject in a situational context.

2. The answer touches on a sensitive subject, causing the respondent to feel reluctant to reveal all. You can in that case use one of three techniques to dig up the required information:

    a) Transpose the subject to a third-person situation ('Imagine you are at a party and you see someone using brand X, what does that tell you about that person?').
    b) Reveal something about yourself, making the respondent feel less inhibited and more likely to share his or her feelings.
    c) Make a note of this problem and come back to it later after you have gathered more information.

When interviewing several respondents about the same domain/customer contact moments, you will notice that some associations are made in nearly all interviews, and that others are only made by one or a small number of respondents. In order to come to a common means–end chain, you will have to set a cut-off point. That means that if you do eight interviews, for example, you choose to only include the associations mentioned by four or more respondents in the common means–end chain. An association that is 'only' made by three respondents will then not be included in this common means–end chain. Where you place that cut-off is wholly arbitrary, but should always be stated in the presentation of your results. You can use Checklist Form 2.2 for the common means–end chain. Note that we have limited ourselves to two columns in this form, meaning that you can record two values here; you can, of course, always modify the form as per the number of values you have tracked down.

CHECKLIST FORM 2.2

Common means–end chain for market/brand _____

Domain/customer contact moment: _____

Number of respondents: _____

Cut-off level used: _____

* * *

Terminal value(s)	_____	_____
Instrumental value(s)	_____	_____
Psycho-social meaning(s)	_____	_____
Functional meaning(s)	_____	_____
Benefit(s)	_____	_____
Feature(s)	_____	_____

Competitor analysis

In the previous steps you have identified internal and possibly also external and potential competitors using the Five Forces Model. Now assess for each competitor what claim they are using to make their brand stick in the target group's minds. Do so by completing Checklist Form 2.3, which categorizes positionings on the basis of the 14 possible approaches outlined in this book.

CHECKLIST FORM 2.3

Positioning approach	Brand	Note
Organization-based		
Corporate ability		
Mentality		
Employee		
Product-based		
Prototypical		
Product features		
Rational benefit		
Marketing-variable-based		
Price		
Distribution		
Design		
Name awareness		
Receiver-based		
Target group		
Situation		
Emotional benefit		
Value		

Notes

1. Myers (1996, pp. 268 and 281) recommends conducting between 30 and 50 interviews in order to be able to draw up a representative number of means–end chains.
2. Reynolds and Gutman (2001).

6
CHOOSING A MARKET POSITION (STEP 5)

Steps 1–4 constituted a major information gathering exercise to underpin the new brand positioning. This last chapter will focus on the actual positioning, i.e. choosing a new market position (Step 5). Section 6.1 will first go into the reasons behind (re)positioning a brand, as well as the different interests at play in that process. Section 6.2 will subsequently focus on the final positioning choice. We will make this final choice by choosing between and within means–end chains, and we will provide a model that can be used to summarize the positioning, the so-called Brand Positioning Sheet (BPS). After having made our positioning choice, Section 6.3 will look into the implications of a new market position for marketing communication in particular. Section 6.4 concludes this chapter and the book with some final considerations for any brand positioning project.

6.1 Reasons for repositioning

In Chapter 1 we have already flagged a number of general developments with repercussions on brand positioning, namely the product, organization and media explosions. In Section 1.3 we pointed out that well-founded brand positioning will have to stand for at least three to four years, and that it is always a good idea to consider repositioning the brand after that period. Apart from this general reason for repositioning a brand, there are also a number of conceivable practical reasons that necessitate repositioning:

- The merger of two organizations or brands: like British Steel and Royal Hoogovens in October 1999, who merged under the pressure of falling steel prices and fierce international competition. The new brand name of the two merged organizations became Corus and was positioned as a global brand with no reference to either country of origin (Britain for

British Steel and the Netherlands for Royal Hoogovens). In 2007 Corus was taken over by the Tata Group, which is originally from India. In the autumn of 2010 the name Corus was replaced by Tata Steel.
- One brand is split up into two or more brands: in Chapter 3 we described the case of a yoghurt and sweet desserts brand; this brand was eventually split up into a desserts brand (Mona) and two yoghurt drink brands (Vifit and Optimel).
- A management buyout in a company, with the new management team looking to present the company differently: in 1989 Arthur Andersen's consultancy wing split from Arthur Andersen and assumed the name Andersen Consulting. They went their own separate ways, with AA ending up a convicted obstructer of justice in the Enron case and AC growing into the world's largest consulting firm after a forced rebranding into Accenture.
- When product innovations cause the old positioning to be found wanting in the highlighting of the product benefits: Sony, for example, has largely failed to claim product innovations in the area of digital music (MP3) and moving images; Apple moved in and took the market with its iTunes/iPod combination.
- Whenever a chosen market position fails to catch on – Coca-Cola Light turned out to be less successful among men, although Coca-Cola Zero subsequently covered this gap – or when a positioning has not managed to draw sufficient attention to the brand.
- When a company wants to launch new products and/or enter new markets (aiming at new target groups): in early 2007 Apple changed its name from Apple Computers Inc. to simply Apple Inc. in order to make it clear to everyone that it not only sells computers.
- When the arrival of new competitors leads to a shift in the target group's perception of the product: in Chapter 4 we referred to the example of Tropicana/Minute Maid, which has been losing out in the freshness perception with the onset of smoothies (most notably those from Innocent Drinks).
- When changes in customer wishes and needs cause a proposition to lose its relevance to the target group: owing to the rise of the Internet, many retailers have been forced to reconsider their positioning. Newspapers that neglected the influence of the Internet on their business are today in severe trouble.

In the first few cases the reason for repositioning is predominantly an internal one; when two companies merge – or when two brands are merged

– the chances are that the former positioning is no longer effective. In the other cases, the reasons are more of an external nature. It is important to realize that there is always some tension between internal and external, whatever the reason for repositioning is. When choosing a market position, one aspect from the BTC model (identity, relevance or differentiation) should never prevail over another. The key is finding a good balance or match amidst these tensions. Figure 6.1 reflects this in a diagram.

As positioning happens amidst the influences exerted by these three aspects, the chances are that the outcome of a positioning process will be some sort of a compromise between the company engendering the brand, the target group that is supposed to buy the brand and the competitors the company is seeking to differentiate the brand from. In Chapter 1 we have already stated that positioning should be *targeted*. This means that you will have to make clear choices on all three of the abovementioned aspects.

With regard to *brand identity*, you will have to define which aspects to highlight and which ones are less suitable for your brand's presentation. Famous retailers like El Corte Ingles and Harrods, for example, sell many different products, but only a small selection of these products are fit for display in the store's shop windows. This does not mean that products that are not on display in the shop window are not sold as much. Displayed products are mainly intended to create a specific image in the market. Car brands do the same by using expensive models in their advertising, while the cheaper models with fewer optional extras actually sell more.

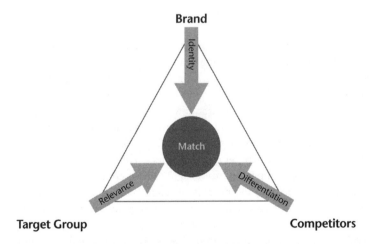

FIGURE 6.1 Positioning is about finding a match between three different aspects

When it comes to the *target group*, you also have to make some tough choices, not only concerning how to target that group, but also what group exactly you will be targeting. Customers will generally not be able to tell you how to present a brand so that they will start finding that brand attractive (otherwise anyone could be an advertising guru or a Harrods shop window designer). It is up to the brand manager – or branding consultant – to pick up on information that could benefit the brand from what target group members say they consider important. Another crucial choice is the choice of target group. By gearing your brand's positioning towards a stereotypical user group, you will be better able to design a brand image. The story goes that the state of Florida started targeting seniors in its communication aimed at tourists; a side effect of this was that the Sunshine State also started attracting more young people.

In the realm of your *competitors*, you also have to make unequivocal choices, not only concerning the actual tactic, but also concerning the competitors you will be offsetting your products against. New brands often tend to stay too closely to the market leader in their positioning. It is a much better idea to emphasize other aspects (Renault can never claim the word 'safety' in the consumer's perception because Volvo has already cornered that market) or even go so far as to designate a new domain. This option was once described as 'The law of the category: if you can't be first in a category, set up a new category you can be first in.'[1] Heineken, for example, struggled to settle in the American market, which was dominated by the big American beer brands; it therefore presented itself as a new beer category, namely that of high-priced import beer. You also have to choose what brands you want to offset yours against. EasyJet possibly considers high-speed rail companies as its main competitors instead of other airlines (because EasyJet's prices are closer to those of high-speed rail companies). Even though two companies can be active in the same market, they are not necessarily each other's competitors.

On the one hand, positioning is intended to create a specific brand image in the market. On the other hand, it is also important to realize that a brand's positioning has to contribute to – or go towards increasing – the brand's ability to be an eye-catching presence in the market. In other words, good positioning makes a brand stand out in the market. Brands with a proven track record in this area are Singapore Airlines, Dell computers and Philips (with its 'Sense and Simplicity' campaign). These companies all succeeded in creating a brand positioning that matched the company, brought the relevance to the target group to the fore and clearly differentiated their brand from competing brands through their message.

Before we go further into the positioning choice, we will clear up two common misconceptions concerning positioning. We have already touched on one in our discussion of the Harrods example. The objective of positioning is for it to add to the product or corporate image. It is therefore more of a management instrument than a sales instrument. But, in practice, that distinction is quite hard to make. Entrepreneurs are often keen to have sales objectives reflected in a positioning. Although sales and marketing have to be on one line, sales objectives do not belong in a positioning process. Examples of successful segregation of marketing and sales are provided by power companies that centre their positioning and communication on energy savings, thus actually encouraging customers to consume less. Another positioning misconception is that choosing a market position is a rational (and quantitatively grounded) process. In Figure 6.1 we pointed out that positioning is all about striking a balance between identity, relevance and differentiation. Because each of these three perspectives is related to a different sphere (own organization, customers and competitors), neither of these spheres will be able to point you in the direction of an effective positioning strategy. By taking the perspectives of the organization, customers and competitors into consideration, a brand manager – or consultant – will find himself able to work out a number of positioning directions. Precisely because this concerns an exploration of the possibilities, a *qualitative assessment* is the most suitable method. At a later stage, there is always the possibility of assessing how the abovementioned spheres view a certain positioning direction. When interpreting the results of such an assessment, you should bear in mind that targeted positioning will both attract and repel people.

6.2 Positioning choice

A Brand Positioning Sheet (BPS) is used to summarize all choices made in the positioning of a brand. Prior to explaining this model, we will first refer back to the means–end chains we outlined in Section 4.2. When determining a brand's positioning, you will have to choose a means–end chain that matches the brand. This will be described further in the following section. After selecting a chain, you will have to choose within that chain those aspects (values, meanings/consequences and/or attributes) that you will place the focus on (see p. 139). The section on p. 147 will wrap things up by showing how to complete a BPS and formulate a brand essence.

Choosing a means–end chain

A means–end chain (ladder) is a string of associative links from values to attributes, via meanings or consequences, and back again from attributes

138 Choosing a market position (Step 5)

to values following the same route. The first choice to make is which means–end chain a brand should tailor to. At this stage it is advisable to take into account what the brand can actually deliver on, what the target group considers relevant and what competitors have not yet claimed.

In the following we will illustrate the means–end chain choice by way of an example we introduced in Chapter 4: secondary school students' university selection drivers. Research has shown that there are two possible means–end chains that can be defined for secondary school students choosing where to enter higher education (see Figure 6.2). The first is driven by the terminal value 'self-fulfilment' and the second by the terminal value 'social recognition'. The meanings and attributes that go with these two terminal values are circled in Figure 6.2.

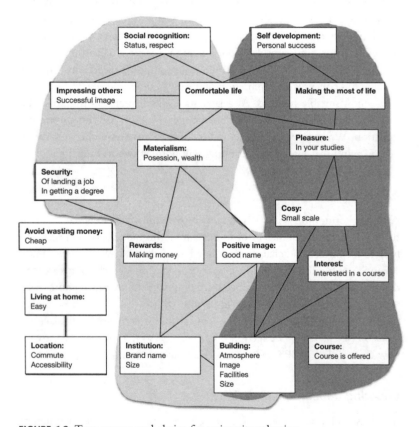

FIGURE 6.2 Two means-end chains for university selection

When choosing one of these means–end chains, from the point of view of a university courting these potential students, you will first have to assess which one best dovetails with the institution's identity. If, for example, a university mainly offers courses with good employment prospects (such as economics, management and law), positioning based on the terminal value 'social recognition' is the obvious choice. Social work or teacher training courses probably better fit the terminal value 'self-fulfilment'. Apart from that, you will also have to evaluate to what extent the university that is positioning itself will be able to use information from these means–end chains to differentiate itself from its competitors.

In the above example we are steering towards the selection of one means–end chain. In practice, positioning often turns out to take elements from two, maybe even three, means–end chains. The number of means–end chains used mostly tallies with the number of selected brand values. For the sake of clarity, we are here working on the assumption that you select one means–end ladder for a brand.

Alongside the choice *between* different means–end chains, you also have to make choices *within* these chains. This takes us to the next step in the positioning choice: selecting the values, meanings/consequences and attributes that you want the brand to respond to.

Choosing values, meanings/consequences and attributes

After having selected a means–end chain to base your positioning on, you go on to determine which aspects from that chain will lead in the positioning and which aspects will serve as secondary support aspects. Two questions or aspects are relevant here:

- Differentiation: to what degree do you want the brand to differentiate itself from the product class and/or differentiate itself from other brands?
- Level: what do you want the positioning to emphasize – brand values, meanings or attributes?

We will elaborate further on these issues below.

Differentiation

There are two possible approaches to 'differentiation': differentiation of the brand with respect to the product class and differentiation with respect to

Choosing a market position (Step 5)

competitors. In previous chapters we have already discussed at length how a brand relates to its product class. In Chapter 4 we covered the 'POP (points of parity)' versus 'POD (points of difference)' issue and in Chapter 5 we introduced the concept 'prototypical positioning'. Chapter 4 also included the MAYA principle, which posits that a brand should always have some connection to the product class in order to be accepted by the target group. The POP versus POD issue necessitates two choices:

1   Will you tie in (either in a positive or a negative sense) with the product class features?
2   If not, how much distance will you maintain between your brand and the typical features of the product class (see Figure 6.3)?

Any final positioning choice is partly about determining how a brand relates to the product class. In Figure 6.3, answering this question starts at the centre of the top of the inverted triangle. When positioning a brand at the POP point, you are basically equating your brand to the product class, and not choosing between and within means–end chains. This leads to a brand coming across as a jack of all trades (and master of none) that is looking to please everyone. In terms of positioning, this is an unwanted situation, because positioning means making choices. You can move away from the POP point by making choices, even when you go for prototypical positioning. Although this approach to positioning means presenting the brand as the prototype of the market, you are still making choices. You are choosing to claim the means–end chain and those values, meanings and attributes that people in that category consider most important. You are, in fact, making a positive

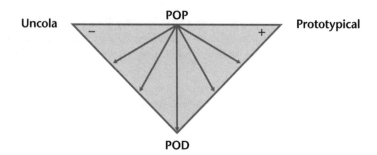

FIGURE 6.3 The field of tension between POP (points of parity) and POD (points of difference)

choice for the essence of the product class, with the brand in question taking on the role of paragon of the category.

You can also emphasize a *negative* relation to the category. This is a relevant tactic when your brand is lacking in some of the essential features of the category. You are then basically only left with the option of 'offsetting' the brand against the category. This way of positioning a brand is also referred to as the 'uncola strategy': 'uncola' is a term coined by the people behind the 7-Up brand, which fiercely tried to differentiate itself from the prototype of soft drinks in the 1970s by stating that it lacked the unique features or ingredients of cola, making it an attractive option for people looking for something different.[2] Although the uncola approach involves you turning your back on the category standard, you are not actually emphasizing POD, because you are still using the associations that people have with the category to present the brand.

In Figure 6.3 we have depicted the deviation from POP in the vertical dimension. The further you descend down the triangle, the fewer POP associations you will be claiming, and the more POD aspects you will be drawing attention to. But this does mean running the risk of making it impossible for customers to fit the product into their mental association schemata by claiming too many POD associations. In Chapter 4 we made reference to the case of the BMW C1, a means of transport that was neither motorcycle nor scooter and that did not require the use of a helmet. POD associations are often needed to draw the brand out of the sphere of jack of all trades and present it as a master in a specific aspect, but this should never be at the expense of alienating the brand from the category. In practice, we often see a combination of POP and POD in positionings.

'Differentiation' should not be limited to weighing up your POPs and PODs. It also involves looking into how and to what extent to draw distinctions with respect to your competitors. The dilemma you are facing here is that fencing your positioning in too much leads you to worry about losing potential customers to a competitor. We cannot reiterate enough that positioning is a marketing tool that is partly intended to increase brand visibility in the market. Apart from marketing, sales have to be generated; sales are greatly aided by people knowing the brand (this builds trust) and having preset, favourable associations with the brand. So it is very important for a brand to succeed in differentiating itself from competing brands. A handy method of determining the extent to which a brand stands out among its competitors is by completing the following sentence: 'Only brand X has . . .'. Research has shown that a challenger choosing the same positioning as the market leader is doomed to be less successful.[3] BMW, for example, chose to change tack in the 1990s and use design in its differentiation strategy with the appointment of American designer Chris Bangle (and later Dutch designer Adriaan van Hooijdonk). This led to BMW managing to knock its arch-rival Mercedes from the top spot of the global ranking of luxury car makers in 2005. BMW's repositioning on the basis of different and innovative design undoubtedly contributed to this rise.

Level

This aspect revolves around the question of what to emphasize in your positioning: brand values, meanings or attributes – or a combination of all three. There are a number of factors that define what you can or must emphasize. We will go over these factors using the 'C-B-M-V model'.[4]

In most markets marketing has become common practice. But these markets have nonetheless gone through a development that you can describe using the C-B-M-V model. Here C-B-M-V stands for 'Characteristics, Benefits, Meanings, Values'. This model describes the development that markets as a whole are undergoing. The fast-moving consumer goods market, for example, saw the creation of the first brands between 1850 and 1900. In those days, brands mostly sought to draw attention to product characteristics in their communication. Decades later, the first companies started to realize that consumers are actually looking for product benefits. In a subsequent development, companies started shifting the focus in their communication onto meanings or values. Pre-World War II cigarette ads, for example, never let up on telling people how well their tobacco tastes (product characteristic experience). Later they started highlighting product benefits, such as the famous Camel ads featuring John Wayne and the zero throat irritation promise.[5] This move was later followed by accentuation of social acceptance (meaning) and finally by communication evoking a certain experience by appealing to one or several values (Camel went for 'adventurous' and Marlboro for 'manliness') up to the moment cigarette advertising was outlawed.

The essence of the above observations is that a provider will have to figure out what stage his market is in (C, B, M or V). In various industrial and business-to-business markets, attributes (characteristics and benefits) still dominate. When all your competitors are for the most part communicating attributes (product characteristics or product benefits), it would not be a good idea to be the only one to emphasize values, because customers will place their 'point of reference' at another position in this model. And when highlighting values in communication has already become common practice in your market, you can go along and do the same, but you can also emphasize attributes. However, the latter is ill advised if all competitors have been communicating values for quite a while already, as any communication-asserting attributes will then not be understood by the market.

In practice, it has turned out that in markets that have gone through the C-B-M-V model you can use all four levels. Apart from choosing one level to focus on, you will then have the option of communicating several levels supporting this leading level. Research has shown that a focus on one or two arguments is most effective, and that communicating values, meanings and attributes around that argument works best to boost the message's credibility.[6] In order to further illustrate this point, we have taken the packaging of Pampers and Huggies in Box 6.1 and Figure 6.4 to show how the full means–end chain is communicated by both these brands, and how differentiation is realized on the level of functional meanings.

When choosing within a means–end chain, you need to select a level to accentuate, as well as levels that will play a supporting role in the communication. This can, for example, mean that you decide to assert a certain value and then use benefits and attributes to substantiate this claim. You can also accentuate attributes and then provide added value for these attributes by connecting them to meanings and (implicitly) referring to values. It is naturally also an option to emphasize meanings and substantiate these with attributes and/or linking them to values.

BOX 6.1 BABY-DRY AND SUPER-FLEX NAPPIES

The product name Baby-Dry refers to the functional meaning of dry baby bottoms and represents the essence of the positioning. As a result, the baby on the packaging is clearly delighted ('happy baby'). The role of the committed mum is also represented on the packaging. And the packaging furthermore communicates a range of symbols for product characteristics (absorbing layers and an elastic closing tape).

Huggies' brand Super-Flex, on the other hand, asserts the functional meaning 'freedom of movement' through both the name and the packaging. Super-Flex packaging depicts the independence of an active baby in an adult world. Here, too, a range of symbols is used to communicate the product characteristics.

144 Choosing a market position (Step 5)

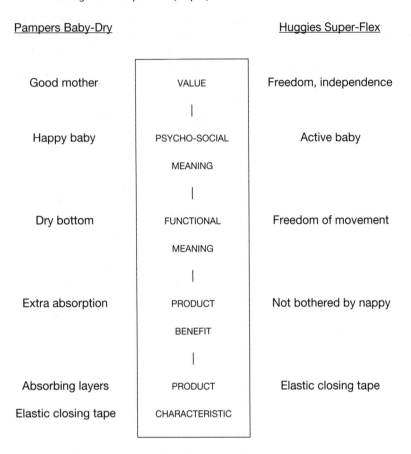

FIGURE 6.4 Means–end chains for two brands of nappies

The question is whether it is advisable for every product to accentuate values. When dealing with a product that, for example, is less important in a consumer's life (low involvement), it is not very useful to position this product on the basis of values. The added value of the product will then not get beyond benefit level for the target group. More important products (high involvement), on the other hand, can be positioned at higher need levels. Take toilet paper, for example, and ask people what they consider important about it. They will all refer to the paper's ability to clean your bottom. When following up on this, they might mention hygiene. And when asked why hygiene is important, they will probably make reference to health. Although there are values to evoke for toilet paper, the question is whether this would actually tempt consumers. The highest need level here is a problem-solving one (clean bottom) and not a problem-preventing one (staying healthy). Baby wipes, such as Pampers' Kandoo wipes, could possibly appeal to the higher level of a problem-preventing need. That is down to fact that parents are always infinitely concerned with the health of their child, which raises their level of involvement. Another example of a product that never makes it past the product benefit level is the battery. Since time eternal, Duracell batteries have been positioned on the basis of the promise that they simply last longer. People's involvement with a product can, however, change with time. Considering our changing lifestyles and the negative consequences that prosperity can bring with it (such as obesity), healthy eating and drinking have steadily become more important to us. Box 6.2 describes the example of Innocent Drinks, a smoothies brand that cleverly tailors to changing consumer concerns. In Table 6.1 we have listed a hypothetical value map for the brand Innocent Drinks.

As we have said, products that are important to consumers can be positioned at higher levels to appeal to higher needs. Such products include those carrying a financial or physical risk or those carrying a personal or social risk. Luxury brands, such as Armani, Gucci and Calvin Klein, are always positioned at a psycho-social meaning level or value level. They are symbols consumers use to shape their own identity.

BOX 6.2 INNOCENT: LITTLE TASTY DRINKS[7]

At the end of the1990s Cambridge graduates Richard Reed, Jon Wright and Adam Balon decided to take the plunge into independent entrepreneurship. In 1998 they spent £500 on fruits to make smoothies, a mixture of pulped and squeezed fruit. They subsequently put up a stall at a London jazz festival, and attracted people's attention with a big sign reading 'Do you think we should give up our day jobs to make these smoothies?' After having one of their smoothies, people could cast their vote by throwing the empty bottle in either the 'Yes' bin or the 'No' bin. At the end of the festival the 'Yes' bin was so full that all three decided to really go ahead and give up their day jobs. The unofficial part of this brand story claims that the 'No' bin contained only three empty bottles, probably deposited by Richard's, Jon's and Adam's mothers.

continued . . .

The success of Innocent Drinks is down to a number of factors. First of all there is the fact that the product constituted a revolutionary U-turn in the juice market: Innocent Drinks uses fresh juice without additives and non-concentrated juice. The idea behind this is that many people live relatively unhealthy lives and that Innocent Drinks can help people improve their eating and drinking habits. Innocent Drinks has pinpointed 'authenticity' as its brand value and impregnates all possible customer contacts with that value. It relentlessly draws attention to the fact that its products consist only of fresh juice without additives. The flagship bottles (250 ml bottles) are transparent; you can tell by the texture of the juice inside that you are buying a fresh product. The relatively high price also helps back up the 'authenticity' claim (one 250 ml bottle will set you back about £1.75 in the UK).

Another unique aspect of Innocent Drinks is the way in which it communicates with its customers. One example of this is the 'bananaphone' – labels on the bottles encourage customers to call Innocent Drinks on a special number, with the call then taken by a random Innocent Drinks staff member. The bananaphone is not specifically intended for comments and/or complaints, but rather so that customers and staff members can have a nice chat. The bananaphone is, in fact, a very clever way of making it clear to people that Innocent Drinks is not some huge inaccessible multinational, but rather a small company with an honest proposition that takes its customers seriously. Another key aspect of Innocent Drinks' communication is the tone of voice, or in the words of Richard Reed himself, 'We take our drinks very seriously, but not ourselves.' This becomes apparent from the texts on their labels, such as 'Innocent smoothies are 54 per cent fruit, 32 per cent fruit, 11 per cent fruit and 3 per cent fruit' and the way they phrase the use-by date: 'Enjoy by . . . (date) . . .'.

This unusual behaviour has helped Innocent Drinks yield impressive operating results. Turnover rose from £0.4m in 1999 to an estimated £115m in 2007 (£1.7m in 2000, £4.1m in 2001, £6.1m in 2002, £10.7m in 2003, £16.7m in 2004, £ 37m in 2005 and £78m in 2006). In 2007 the company sold over 2 million bottles a week! In April 2009 Innocent Drinks sold a 20 per cent stake to the US corporate giant The Coca-Cola Company.

TABLE 6.1 Possible means–end chain for Innocent Drinks

Terminal values	Authenticity (not fake); fun (not aimed at easing a sense of guilt)
Instrumental values	Honesty
Psycho-social meaning	'Makes me feel good'; 'I'm letting others know I'm looking after my health'
Functional meaning	'Is healthy'; 'Very tasty'
Product benefits	'Real taste'; 'Not a bulk product from an inaccessible multinational'
Product features	100% fruit without additives; transparent 250 ml bottles; relatively high price; ingredients guide; 'bananaphone' number

Completing a Brand Positioning Sheet (BPS)

A BPS (see Figure 6.5) logs all choices made in a positioning process. It is made up of the following nine elements, with the first three relating to the pre-positioning analysis and the remaining six to the positioning choice:

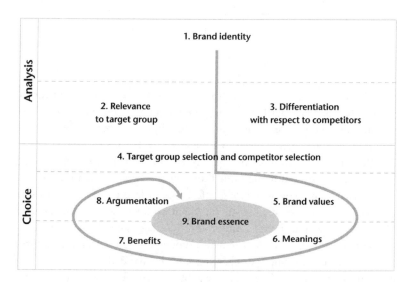

FIGURE 6.5 Blank version of a Brand Positioning Sheet

1. Brand identity: this is where you summarize what the brand is by listing all identity aspects (regardless of their relevance to the customer). You should pay special attention to (conclusions regarding) the corporate identity and (conclusions regarding) brand architecture.
2. Relevance to the target group: this section allows you to record how all attributes are relevant or mean something to a target group, as well as which values can be linked to these meanings.
3. Differentiation with respect to competitors: list the attributes, meanings/consequences and values that can set the brand apart from competing brands here.

The first three steps can be covered simultaneously by running a means–end analysis for the market using the laddering technique (see Section 4.2). You should try to be as detailed as possible when mapping all attributes, meanings/consequences and values. Only after having done that do you start making choices:

4. Target group selection and competitor selection: this requires you choosing which target group you want to focus your advertising on (such as Florida's elderly tourists) and which market parties you consider to be your competitors (such as EasyJet identifying high-speed rail as its main competitor). In all subsequent choices you will have to take these two groups as your starting point.
5. Brand values: as part of the positioning process you will be selecting two or three brand values from all possible values. Brand values can be embodied through personification, the description of the brand identity in personality features or character traits.
6. Meanings (or consequences): this is where you choose the functional and/or psycho-social meanings the brand will be eliciting. These meanings constitute, in fact, the reasons why people buy the brand; they are therefore often referred to as *consumer* or *customer insights*.
7. Benefits: this section is where you record the benefits you will be using in the brand communication. From all the benefits identified in the analysis phase, you will choose a few that fit in the brand's means–end chain. In the case of a low-involvement product, two or three benefits will suffice, and there is some room for exaggeration (over-claiming); in the case of a high-involvement product you can stretch this to three to four benefits, but over-claiming must be avoided.[8]
8. Argumentation: this is made up of the concrete product features you will be deploying to convince the target group that the brand is

the best choice for them. The features you select are the so-called reasons to believe.

After having gone through steps 5–8, you would do well in trying to summarize the ensuing positioning in one word or one short sentence:

9   Brand essence: an inspiring, clear-cut and guiding sentence that sums up the brand's positioning. This sentence is sometimes referred to as the 'brand mantra'.[9] The brand essence is usually not used in external communication; it is a short phrase that is only used by managers who are involved with the brand (it is not a tagline or a pay-off). In Box 6.3 you will find an example of a brand essence for the brand Nike.

BOX 6.3 THE NIKE BRAND ESSENCE[10]

Nike evokes a rich set of associations in its customers, such as innovative product design, sponsoring of sports stars, award-winning advertising campaigns, and its competitive drive and singular attitude. Marketing management uses a three-word brand essence internally to ensure that all staff members are singing off the same hymn sheet: *authentic athletic performance*. All of Nike's marketing activities, including the products and the way they are advertised and sold, have to harness the brand values of this brand essence. The choice for this brand essence is considered an intellectual brand compass intended to ensure that the brand stays on track. All new products and product line extensions have to be sufficiently innovative in their use of materials, fit and design to make them truly meaningful for top athletes. Product design at Nike has also developed along the brand essence line. The meaning of Nike as a brand has grown from 'running shoes' to 'athletic shoes' and subsequently to 'athletic shoes and apparel' to 'all things associated with athletics'. Every step in this development was driven by the brand mantra: authentic athletic performance. Past fiascos were mostly down to Nike swaying from the brand essence. A line of outdoor shoes and clothing, for example, flopped horribly because the competitive aspect that is locked in the brand essence is less pertinent to the use of such products.

Apart from completing the BPS, it is also a good idea to sum up your brand positioning in a few sentences (a so-called brand positioning statement). This statement will highlight the *choices* you have made along the way. Box 6.4 contains the positioning statement we have formulated to match the Innocent Drinks case described in Box 6.2. Your positioning statement can vary depending on the approach used for the means–end chain. The example in Box 6.4 is based on the brand values of Innocent Drinks. We have chosen a target group of 25- to 35-year-olds for this example, because people in this age bracket will have the spending power to afford the relatively expensive smoothies, will have busy jobs not allowing them the time to always eat healthy food, and, in contrast to older people, will still be willing to try out new products. (For the sake of completeness, we should point out that this is a fictitious example.)

BOX 6.4 POSITIONING STATEMENT FOR INNOCENT DRINKS (FICTITIOUS)

Innocent Drinks [brand name] is a brand of smoothies [product description] targeting young consumers (25–35 years of age) with relatively unhealthy eating and drinking habits, and who want to compensate for that in an easygoing and voluntary way [target group].

Innocent Drinks stresses at every occasion that its products are 100 per cent natural (authentic) and do not seek to tune into people's sense of guilt about not eating healthily, and on top of that the company communicates with its customers in an honest and relaxed manner [brand values].

Innocent Drinks wants to make its customer feel good through its products, to offer them the opportunity to show others they take their health seriously, and to be associated with both healthy and tasty [meanings/consequences].

The values and meanings of Innocent Drinks have to come to the fore in the fact that its smoothies are 100 per cent fruit without additives, and that consumers do not experience it as a mass product made by an inaccessible multinational [attributes].

Innocent Drinks stands out among its competitors by emphasizing authenticity and informality through humour [competitive differentiation].

Based on the above positioning statement, Innocent Drinks' brand essence could be 'Real fruit juice that lends colour to your life'.

With the formulation of a positioning statement, the course for the brand is set. New positioning can have major implications for the brand, not only in terms of communication, but also for the product. On the basis of the positioning, one should choose which products should be focused on in communication (and which products not). The positioning may also set directions for new-product development, as is the case for Apple, for example. In the next section we will mainly focus on the implications of the new positioning for communication.

6.3 Communicative realization

Completing a BPS is no easy task. And after you have managed it, you will face an even tougher challenge: communicative realization of the chosen positioning. Positioning basically has two communication objectives: boosting brand awareness and evoking the right brand name associations. Before we elaborate upon these two objectives, we will discuss the Brand Circle, a model that may help you to decide which products from the brand can best be used to bring the positioning across.

Choosing the products that may bring the positioning across

Although one-product brands do exist, most brands carry several products. Take car brands, for example, which carry a range of different models and types of cars. While it is true that brand positioning does not necessarily have to hinge on products, the fact is that some products better incarnate a positioning than others. To make this seemingly rather abstract matter a little more concrete, you only need to put yourself in the shoes of the window dresser at Harrods. It is his or her job to decide which products to use in Harrods' window displays. The products on display in its windows largely determine Harrods' brand image, with exclusive and exotic products matching that image best. But there are, of course, also numerous products that, owing to a mismatch with the Harrods brand image, never make it into Harrods' elaborate window displays, but that Harrods probably does sell. Every brand must look at this issue: which products make for good display items, and which don't? In other words, which products help build the desired brand image, and which don't? It would even be good to answer the question of which products actually detract from the desired brand image.

152 Choosing a market position (Step 5)

The Brand Circle (see Figure 6.6) is a handy model that provides insight into how products relate to the brand image and can help brand managers decide which products to use in brand expressions.[11]

In the *Brand Circle* four areas are defined that are relevant for bringing a positioning across:

1. Inner core: this where the core products of a brand are located, products that encapsulate the brand positioning. These tend to be the products the brand uses to present itself in the market. The inner core is basically part of the brand's DNA, and hence decisive for the answer to the question what the brand in essence stands for. In the case of a soft drinks brand these could be the main flavours offered by the brand.
2. Outer core: this is where products are located that match (part of) the brand positioning, but that are not as suited for use in attempts to raise the brand's market profile. These products are mostly sparked by new market demand, and not introduced as a way of broadening the brand on the basis of the brand essence. A brand of carbonated soft drinks, for example, could choose to launch a 'no bubbles' version of another one of its soft drinks, as a way of tailoring to people who dislike fizzy drinks.

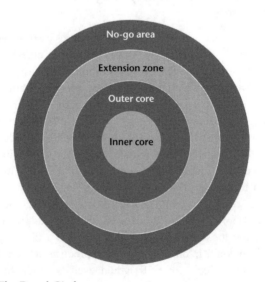

FIGURE 6.6 The Brand Circle

3   Extension zone: this is the area of a brand's latent potential. This includes brand and concept extensions. Brand extensions are products that take the brand into a new product category, different from the products from the inner core, but still of the same product type. For example, ice cream by Mars falls into another product category than Mars bars, but both are still the same type of product (i.e. food). Concept extensions are totally different products that do not relate to the brand on a product level (such as Caterpillar shoes and Caterpillar machines). Extension-zone products will most likely be stored in different mental schemes, thereby not affecting the image of the original branded product (see also the discussion on Harley-Davidson aftershave in Box 3.3).

4   No-go area: this is where we find products that actually may harm the brand. The idea is, of course, to avoid introducing products in this outermost circle, but it is always advisable to identify possible products that would take the brand into this 'no-go area' in order to know what not to go for. As shown in Box 3.3, Harley-Davidson should preferably not try to attach its name to a scooter.

Now we have identified which products can best effectuate a brand's chosen positioning in the market, we can turn to the question how the chosen positioning can best be put across in advertising and other communication.

Boosting brand awareness

Marketing science – as well as marketing practice – makes little reference to the concept of brand awareness. In our opinion, this is one of the most underrated aspects of building a brand. The scanty research on the subject has shown that people think that products from well-known brands are better than those from lesser-known brands, and that simply raising brand awareness has a strong positive impact on the quality perception people have of brand products. One study even came to the conclusion that a brand's market share is 70 per cent down to brand awareness and 'only' 30 per cent down to actual associations.[12] We can therefore safely say that 'unknown, unloved' really applies, and that we cannot afford to neglect brand awareness.

We have stressed the importance of targeted positioning on various occasions in this book, since positioning has to contribute to the brand's visibility and ability to catch the consumer's eye. Yet not all brands need to strive for a high degree of spontaneous brand awareness. In some cases *assisted* brand awareness will suffice. In order to explain this nuance, we will first go over the four categories of brand awareness (Figure 6.7).

154 Choosing a market position (Step 5)

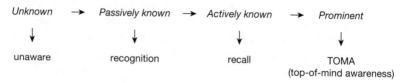

FIGURE 6.7 Four brand awareness categories

The first brand awareness category we can distinguish is that of *unawareness*. In practice, this will hardly ever occur; only new brand launches will face total unawareness in the early stages. Many of the brands out there are *passively known* to us; when people are asked to look at a list of petrol companies (such as Avia, BP, Fina, Esso, Shell, Q8, Repsol, Tamoil, Texaco, and Total) and to say whether they know them, they will probably answer 'Yes' for each brand. In other words, many people will *recognize* these brands. Recognition is also referred to as 'assisted recall'; people have heard of the name and/or logo, but will mostly be unable to actively recall the name when you ask them to list petrol companies. When you ask someone to list as many petrol companies as possible, most will probably only *recall* BP, Esso and Shell (i.e. *active awareness/recognition*). The brand that people tend to come up with first in answering the above question is the most *prominent* brand, i.e. the brand with 'top-of-mind awareness' (TOMA). In the case of petrol companies this is most likely to be the company that has the most petrol stations in that country.

An important aspect of positioning is knowing what level of awareness among consumers corresponds to your brand. As there will always be differences between consumers where recognition and recall are concerned, the following criteria to chart brand awareness levels provide rough, not exact, insight:

- If no more than 20 per cent of potential consumers mention brand X spontaneously, the brand is basically *unknown*.
- If more than 20 per cent but fewer than 40 per cent of potential consumers mention brand X spontaneously, the brand is *relatively unknown*.
- If more than 40 per cent but fewer than 70 per cent of potential consumers mention brand X spontaneously, the brand is *relatively well known*.
- If more than 70 per cent of potential consumers mention brand X spontaneously, the brand is very *well known*.

It is important to realize that the benefits of brand policy-making only start to kick in when over 70 per cent of potential customers manage to mention the brand spontaneously. Their high brand awareness level leads these kinds of brands to inspire confidence without prodding consumers. Brands that have attained this status are called 'trusted brands'. Brands with a level of brand awareness of over 90 per cent are 'iconic brands'; these are the brands that have become part of our culture.

Although a high level of brand awareness is key for the success of a brand, we still have to bring in some nuance here. For products whose brand is not immediately visible at the places where they are sold, active brand awareness is an absolute must. In a bar, when searching the Internet or in a retail outlet where there is no self-service (such as a chemist's), consumers will have to be able to recall the brand names of products they are looking for. Active brand recognition is also of vital importance for service providers and business-to-business companies. In other purchasing situations people will see the brands they can choose from, such as when choosing between fast-moving consumer goods at the supermarket or between durable consumer goods. In such situations it will, in principle, be enough for the brand to merely be *recognized*. Although in our view active awareness is always better for a brand than passive awareness, it may be required for budgetary reasons to aim for brand recognition instead of brand recall.

When aiming for brand recognition, a provider will have to be mindful of the following:[13]

- A link must be established between the brand and the product class in each communication (the mental link between product class and brand is crucial here). By having a tagline (a few words or a descriptive sentence) accompany the brand name, it will be clear what kind of product goes with the brand (as Lloyds does with the tagline 'the world's leading insurance market').
- All communication has to clearly show the brand and/or packaging, as well as the logo (two seconds is enough in TV ads).
- The logo should be easy to remember. People will be more likely to remember logos when:[14]
    - they represent real objects (Shell, WWF);
    - they are 'organic', with curves (Nike, McDonald's);
    - they are nearly symmetrical (British Rail);
    - they have internal repetition (British Rail, McDonald's).

For a new brand, or after repositioning a brand, the provider will have to launch a high-frequency advertising campaign in the beginning, with the frequency being lowered at a later stage (for 'maintenance').

When aiming for *brand recall*, a provider will have to take the following into consideration:

- The link to the product class is a less important aspect of communication than when aiming for recognition. After all, the brand name is the primary point of entry to the associative network in the mind in the case of brand recall. It is important for the communication to highlight the link between the brand and (associations with) the differentiating attributes.
- Recall can be increased by using a brand ambassador. This can be done by having someone present the brand in ads, the way George Clooney presents Nespresso in Europe and Pierce Brosnan L'Oréal's line for aging men. Recall can also be reinforced by jingles, pictures or striking associations.
- Brands needing brand recall to be able to be successful have to be advertising with high frequency all the time.

We can conclude from this that brand awareness is of paramount importance for the financial and economic success of a brand. The positioning chosen for a brand will most certainly have to contribute to the brand's presence – and hence people's awareness of the brand. Active brand name awareness is indispensable for brands that are not always visible at places where they are sold – or at the moments people need the product. In some cases it is a valid option to aim for passive awareness. Apart from brand awareness, it is also important for the positioning to call up certain brand associations in people.

Evoking brand associations

Besides being eye-catching, a positioning also has to make the brand one that receivers will form the desired brand image with. By emphasizing specific associations, the brand will carve out a differentiating and possibly unique position in the mind of the receiver. The communication method determines to a significant degree whether such associations are or are not linked to the brand. The communication grid in Table 6.2 enables you to figure out how to communicate the right associations. The basis of this grid is formed by two dimensions (purchase motivation and involvement), leading to four quadrants.

TABLE 6.2 Communication grid based on motivation for purchase and involvement[15]

		Negative ('must')	Positive ('lust')
Involvement	Low	• Medicine • Low-calorie beer • Laundry detergents • Routinely used industrial products	• Soft drinks • Beer (regular ~) • Snacks and desserts • Cosmetics
	High	• Housing • Professional calculators • Insurance policies • New industrial products	• Holidays • Fashion • Cars • Corporate image
		Purchase motivation	

Source: Reproduced with permission from J.R. Rossiter and S. Bellman, *Marketing Communications: Theory and Applications*. © 2005 Pearson Australia (p. 152, Figure 8.1).

Communication grid

The communication grid in Table 6.2 is based on two dimensions: type of purchase motivation (negative versus positive) and degree of involvement (low versus high). The idea is to assess which of the four quadrants your brand fits into.

Where purchase motivation is concerned, you can make a further distinction between a negative and a positive reason for buying a brand:

- Negative motivation is when you buy a certain brand product to solve a problem or prevent it from occurring in the first place, or to solve or prevent an undesired situation. The products that you buy for negative reasons are 'must' products; they are products you cannot do without if you want to tackle a problem, such as cleaning products and detergent (problem prevention), medicine, but also insurances, and even education to a certain degree.
- Positive motivation is when you buy a brand product for the sake of pleasure (alcoholic drinks or ice cream), for intellectual stimulation (a thrilling book) or to acquire social recognition (cars). The products in question are 'lust' products; they are products you could easily live without, but by using them you are adding a dimension to your life.

You are largely free to decide what motivations to focus on. Many brand products could tailor to either a negative or a positive motivation; it is up to you, as the brand manager, to decide which purchase motivation to tie in with. A university, for example, could choose to appeal to a negative motivation by stressing in their communication that career prospects are seriously hampered, or even wiped out altogether, when you do not attain a university degree. Or they could go for a positive motivation by emphasizing the intellectual challenge offered by their courses. Depending on the characteristics of the product and the motivation you wish to appeal to, the level of involvement is likely to change. Before we go into this any further, we will briefly outline the concept of involvement.

Evaluating consumer involvement means assessing whether that consumer thinks purchasing the product constitutes a high or a low risk. This is basically all about perceived risk. There are two drivers behind perceived risk that determine whether consumers have high or low involvement with a brand:

1. High involvement exists when the perceived *financial and economic* risk upon purchasing a brand product is high. This risk is expressed in terms of money, but also exists when people feel they are running the risk of having purchased a product that does not function the way it should, when there is a possible danger to personal safety or health, or when the purchase can lead to time wastage or inconvenience.
2. High involvement is also achieved when the perceived *psycho-social* risk incurred by buying a brand product is high. This can be the case when buying products that are supposed to match people's self-image (such as clothes) and/or have to be approved by friends or family (such as cars).

Almost all high-priced brand products have high levels of consumer involvement. Low-priced brand products can reach high levels of involvement when purchase leads the buyer to incur a psycho-social risk (for example, with clothes or fashion accessories).

As a brand manager, you can choose freely which kind of purchase motivation you want the brand to appeal to. Depending on your choice, the level of involvement is subsequently subject to change. A consumer can, for example, buy a fat-free dessert for a negative reason (diet) or a positive reason (good taste). In the case of positive motivation involvement will be low, and in the case of negative motivation it will be high (such as when excess weight is causing psycho-social problems).

The choice of the type of purchase motivation the communication will tie in with can have major consequences in terms of product acceptance

Choosing a market position (Step 5) **159**

and success. In Boxes 6.5 and 6.6 we give two examples demonstrating the difference this choice can make. First, OMO, Unilever's biggest fabric-cleaning brand, changed the focus from a negative motivation to a positive motivation with the launch of the 'Dirt is good' campaign. Second, Box 6.6 demonstrates these differences using the example of Shell, which replaced the unsuccessful fuel Pura (with a negative motivation for purchase) by V-Power (with a positive motivation for purchase).

The example of Shell's forays into petrol with a twist shows that targeting a positive or a negative purchase motivation can make all the difference. Although this example focuses on the shift in target from negative to positive

---

BOX 6.5 'DIRT IS GOOD'[16]

In 2006 the OMO Global Brand Team set off on a journey to accelerate the growth of Unilever's biggest fabric-cleaning brand into a single consolidated global umbrella philosophy. Known variously to consumers around the world as OMO, Persil, Skip or ALA, Unilever's laundry brand, with revenues well over US$2 billion, has evolved from a loose confederation of brands with over 25 widely differing positions, names and packaging designs, to a strong global brand under the single global umbrella of 'Dirt is Good' ('DIG'). This consolidation under the DIG umbrella, with a new winning brand development strategy and world-class marketing mix, has successfully challenged traditional market beliefs, and put the competition on the defensive.

Other laundry brands work on the commonsense principle of removing stains and dirt. DIG, however, turned this traditional perception on its head. DIG is committed to encouraging parents to leave their children free to get dirty, on the basis that it is through experiencing life at first hand that children learn and so develop. The ultimate benefit that DIG is aiming to offer as a brand is child development. The brand addresses this universal consumer need, which is intrinsically connected to the brand itself. DIG also offers a solution to this need by raising awareness and promoting outside play and interaction with nature, with mothers not needing to worry, because DIG's laundry products will be there to pick up the pieces.

BOX 6.6 SHELL PURA VERSUS SHELL V-POWER

During the year 2000 in several countries, Shell launched a new type of petrol. In the Netherlands this was done under the name Shell Pura. Pura was a cleaner, further developed petrol containing fewer contaminants than regular petrol, making it more environmentally friendly as well as better for car engines. It was the first time that Shell had introduced environmentally friendly petrol next to its 'regular' petrol. Research had shown that consumers were willing to pay a price premium for cleaner petrol. The name Pura appealed to ideas of purity and cleanliness for both the environment and the engine. Shell appealed to people's sense of guilt about polluting the environment and offered them 'redemption'. On top of that, Pura also claimed a role in preventing problems caused by a dirty engine. Shell Pura was clearly targeting several *negative* motivations for purchase. Moreover, it was also targeting *collective* motivations for purchase: to reduce emission and work on a cleaner environment for everyone. Shell Pura was about 9 eurocents more expensive than Euro 95 petrol. But Pura never turned into the success Shell had envisaged. Even though earlier market research had indicated that people were willing to pay a premium for environmentally friendly petrol, in reality this turned out not to be the case. Further research showed that people who did buy Shell Pura did not buy it because of environmental claims, but because it was indeed better for the engine and therefore cost-efficient. In 2004, Shell Pura was replaced by Shell V-Power.

Shell's claims for V-Power include that it is a fuel with a positive effect on engine power. V-Power appeals to positive motivations for purchase, such as the feeling of power and the impression you want to make on others. Also, instead of targeting the collective motivations for purchase such as a cleaner environment, it is targeting *individualistic* motivations of purchase: a cleaner engine, more power and saving on costs. In contrast to the blue of Pura, V-Power uses feisty red and gives you the feeling you are 'putting a Ferrari in your engine'. The motivation for buying V-Power also ties in with the motivations underlying people's car buying and ownership behaviour (namely freedom and driving enjoyment).

Although Shell Pura and Shell V-Power are both differentiated fuels, they have distinct formulations and specifications. Where Pura cut

continued . . .

sulphur emissions by 55 per cent, V-Power is completely sulphur-free. Shell Pura's engine purifying qualities, which many drivers considered to be its strong point, were further improved in Shell V-Power. When launched in 2004, V-Power cost 4.5 eurocents more than the recommended retail price for Euro 95 petrol. In the end, positioning on a positive and individualistic, instead of a negative and collectivistic, motivation for purchase turned out to make an important difference. In 2009 Shell introduced Shell Fuelsave. According to Shell, this type of petrol is more efficient than other types; it can save up to a litre per tank, which makes it more cost-efficient. With this type of petrol, Shell is again targeting a positive and individualistic purchase motivation.

Shell Pura

Shell V-Power

Shell FuelSave

motivation, this does not mean that stressing a positive purchase motivation always yields greater success. But the example does show that your choice of purchase motivation to target is a key one, and one that can make or break the product.

Creative guidelines

Research in the field of advertising has over the years yielded various guidelines for communication within the communication grid. These guidelines are summarized in Table 6.3.

Cluster brands (negative motivation for purchase, low involvement) require an emphasis on the simple depiction of how the brand can solve problems. Ensuing communication will present a problem, with the brand product saving the day and solving that problem ('Filthy kitchen floor? Cillit Bang and bye bye dirt!'). Research has shown that these types of ads do not have to be clever and enjoyable to be effective; in other words, 'likeability' is not a prerequisite for effectiveness here. Owing to their low level of involvement,

TABLE 6.3 Creative guidelines for advertising[17]

Involvement	Negative motivation for purchase	Positive motivation for purchase
Low	Cluster brand: • Simple presentation of problem-solving quality • People don't have to like these ads • Only highlight one or two benefits • Extreme benefit claims are OK • Benefits have to stick	Territory brand: • Authentic emotionalism ('ring true') • Emotion used has to be unique to the brand • Target group has to like these ads • No explicit communication of the brand's usefulness (only through association) • Repetition has a build-up and reinforcement function
High	Information brand: • Correct emotional presentation • Target group has to accept main points of the message • People don't have to like these ads • Initial attitude of the target group is very important • Aim high in the claims (but do not over-claim) • Claims have to be convincing • Counter possible objections • Possibly: comparative advertising	Mythical brand: • Authentic emotionalism • Target group has to like these ads • Target group has to identify with the brand • Some information can be useful (risk reduction) • Over-claiming is OK (never under-claim) • Repetition has a build-up and reinforcement function

receivers will not be willing to take in a great deal of information about this kind of brand product. So there is only room to highlight one or two benefits. But this can be done with some level of exaggeration to attract people's attention; extreme claims in communication are allowed here (we can all remember detergent ads with extremely stubborn stains made on clothes, which detergent X subsequently makes disappear, leaving clothes looking like new). The receiver will have to remember the presented benefits with ease, so they cannot be too complicated. Because receivers do not process the messages from this kind of product with great intensity, there is even the option of using irrelevant attributes. One classic example of that is offered by an American instant coffee brand that claims its instant coffee granules are crystal-shaped ('flaked coffee crystals'), and then goes on to claim that this benefits the taste of the coffee. Subsequent research confirmed that consumers actually do think that the crystal shape of the granule makes the coffee taste better, even after they have heard coffee experts state that this argument does not wash.[18]

For *information brands* (negative motivation for purchase, high involvement) your communication will have to focus on transmitting a number of claims or arguments. Because you are dealing with high levels of involvement here, receivers will pay closer attention to the message and its arguments than they do in the case of cluster brands. It is important here that the target group accepts the main points of the message. This means that over-claiming is out of the question, and that claims should be at a high level. Claims have to be convincing, which you can reinforce by also providing counter-arguments alongside your arguments in favour of the brand. This means anticipating possible objections people could have against the brand product and refuting them. It is essential in the case of information brands to be well aware of the target group's initial attitude and to tie in with that. You will also regularly have to 'refresh' a message; when the target group is presented with the same arguments too long, they can develop an aversion to the brand. Furthermore, 'likeability' is not strictly necessary here. Receivers' high level of involvement and their extensive knowledge of what's on offer in the market gives information brands the option to use comparative advertising. But be aware of the fact that this kind of advertising is subject to all sorts of rules and conditions. Comparative advertising offers an easy way of making it clear to people how a brand differs from competing brands. Comparative advertising is mostly used to stress the competitor's weaknesses. In the 2004 presidential election race in the USA, comparative advertising was used to enfeeble the competition's strengths (see Box 6.7). But in the case of most products and services, we would advise against using this strategy, because it does not show the brand in a positive light.

In the case of *territory brands* (positive motivations for purchase, low involvement) the communication has to focus on finding and transmitting a unique and authentic (real) emotion. Receivers are here generally not so much interested in information about the brand product, but rather after a feel-good factor emitted by the communication (in contrast to products with a negative purchase motivation, brand products with a positive purchase motivation do depend on the likeability factor). So there is no need to explicitly communicate the usefulness of the brand, although you can still

BOX 6.7 SWIFTBOATING

The term 'swiftboating' is used in American politics to refer to an action by which a politician attempts to discredit his opponent on his (supposed) strengths. The term was coined in 2004 when the democratic presidential candidate John Kerry tried to defeat the incumbent George W. Bush, who ended up winning the election and staying on for a second term.

During the campaign, John Kerry often boasted about his past as a soldier in the Vietnam War. He claimed to have been a swiftboater, part of a military unit using fast boats (swift boats) to strike against the Viet Cong in the Mekong River Delta. Kerry supposedly performed heroics in several confrontations with the enemy, and even single-handedly evacuated wounded fellow soldiers. Kerry was awarded a Bronze Star, a Silver Star and as many as three Purple Hearts.

During the 2004 presidential campaign, Kerry endured fierce criticism from around 200 Vietnam veterans calling themselves the 'Swift Boat Veterans for Truth' (SBVT). These veterans called Kerry's account of his heroics in Vietnam into question, and asked whether he really merited all the medals he was awarded. The SBVT, in turn, was accused of working under the orders of George W. Bush and his aide and campaign strategist Karl Rove.

do so implicitly by using associative techniques. In ads for beer brewed using mineral water you can do this by showing a crystal-clear stream in the background. This form of communication can be repeated more often than the communication used for products that are bought for negative reasons. Repetition of ads has a build-up and reinforcing effect here.

For *mythical brands* (positive motivation for purchase, high involvement) your communication will have to focus on transmitting an authentic emotion. With a certain level of exaggeration, we can say that this calls for advertising that would have to make receivers feel all 'warm inside' upon first seeing it. This effect can be achieved by using certain music, or with images. A good example is Levi's 501 legendary 'Launderette' TV commercial (1985). By referencing to the roaring fifties, Levi's tapped into history, continuity and vintage chic with this TV commercial – starring model, actor and pop singer Nick Kamen. In the video Kamen walks into a launderette to the tune of

Marvin Gaye's 'I Heard It Through the Grapevine' and empties a bag of rocks into the washing machine. He strips down to his boxer shorts, putting his clothes into the washer while the other people in the laundromat watch in surprise. The end line says, 'The original shrink-to-fit jeans' and 'Now available stonewashed.'[19] Because mythical brands come with a high level of target group involvement, it can be useful to provide some information. But it is then important that this information appeal to (feelings of) risk reduction. As with territory brands, repetition has a build-up and a reinforcing effect here.

6.4 Closing remarks

Recategorization

Most positioning processes consist of the repositioning of existing brands rather than the introduction of completely new ones. When repositioning, many brands will find it hard to shake a deeply ingrained brand image, as we pointed out in Chapter 4. This basically calls for drastic brand recategorization in the minds of consumers. Most telephone companies, for example, decided to embark on a major recategorization of their brand – from telecommunication provider to a triple player (telecommunications, Internet and TV). Recategorization of a brand involves consumers learning new brand associations, as well as unlearning certain set associations. In practice, it turns out that people have greater difficulty unlearning old associations than learning new ones. Apart from communication, there are a number of other ways of changing the mental associative network around a brand. We list here those that are the most commonly used:

- Changing the brand name. This is only a valid strategy if the name itself carries negative associations.
- Changing the visual brand identity. This strategy is particularly effective when the current visual identity is outdated. Depending on the level of change, the impact on people's associative thinking patterns relating to the brand can be major or minor; the final effects of such a change will in any case only be visible in the medium to long term.
- Introducing a new product under the brand name in question (an 'extension'). This strategy can change the mental associative network around a brand right away, as it adds new associations and (slowly) elbows out old ones. Porsche used to be known for its 911 model, a sports car introduced in 1963, which had the archetypical Porsche shape. In 2002

Porsche launched the Cayenne, a sports utility vehicle that hardly resembles the 911 at all. The Cayenne has undoubtedly changed Porsche's brand image as a sports car maker, even more so considering the Cayenne currently generates 70 per cent of Porsche's turnover.
- Linking up with another brand product. This strategy is known as 'co-branding'. Another brand can bring in new associations for the brand in question, leading to quick changes in consumers' mental image of the brand. Philips pulled this off by marketing a kitchen appliances range together with Alessi. When ending a co-branding venture, both parties involved will have to be careful not to undo all the realized effects.

Consistency

The main ingredient of the realization of strong market positioning is consistency. All instances and methods of contact between the brand and its target group have to be perfectly harmonized. The use of the brand has to meet the expectations raised in the brand communication. This goes both for the use of physical products and the experience consumers have when dealing with staff when consuming services. The design of products, packaging, buildings, shops, uniforms, logos, etc. has to dovetail with the communication and the products. This consistency of all deployed brand identity drivers seems logical, but we often see brands failing to attain that level of integration. There is therefore still a lot of ground to be gained in this area.

With these closing remarks we have come to the end of this book. We have chronicled the ins and outs of 'positioning' on the basis of the selection process that you, as the brand manager, have to complete to position your brand. And in doing that we have given this subject a new twist by stressing the relevance of the inside-out perspective (without detracting from the outside-in approach), by showing that choices in the area of brand architecture have consequences for positioning, and by detailing new analysis techniques to unleash on the target group and competitors. What we have most sought to impart is that the bottom line of positioning is the need to make razor-sharp choices.

Notes

1 Ries and Trout (1986). See also Kim and Mauborgne's (2005) ideas on moving from a 'red' to a 'blue ocean'.
2 Ries and Trout (2006, p. 127); Sengupta (2005, pp. 10ff).
3 Rossiter and Bellman (2005, p.144).

Choosing a market position (Step 5)   167

4 This model is described by Rossiter and Bellman (2005, pp. 71ff) as the 'A-B-E benefit claim model', with 'A' standing for 'attributes', 'B' for 'benefits' and 'E' for 'emotions'. We have chosen to stretch this model to four terms to tie it in with the terms used for means–end chains. See also Rossiter and Percy (2001).
5 For more examples, see http://graphic-design.tjs-labs.com/table-view.php?advertiser=r★★j★★reynolds★tobacco★co★ (accessed 9 February 2011).
6 Research by Roth (1992). See also Reynolds and Craddock (2001).
7 Riezebos (2007).
8 Rossiter and Bellman (2005, pp. 168ff).
9 Keller et al. (2008, pp. 118ff).
10 From Keller et al. (2008, p. 124).
11 Davidson (1987). See also Kapferer (2008).
12 Miller and Berry (1998).
13 Rossiter and Bellman (2005).
14 Henderson and Cote (1998).
15 This model is based on the so-called Rossiter, Percy and Bellman grid (Rossiter and Bellman, 2005, pp. 151ff).
16 Based on 'Unlocking OMO's Global Brand Potential'. Source: www.effectivebrands.com (accessed 30 December 2010).
17 The creative guidelines were sourced from Rossiter and Bellman (2005, Chapter 8). The names for the four different brand types are from Van Kralingen (1999, p. 297).
18 Carpenter et al. (1994).
19 Source: Facebook Page of Levi's 501 Jeans.

APPENDIX A

Brand Key Model[1]

The Brand Key Model is a model that can be used to position brands. This model is used in a range of different organizations, comes in different shapes and sizes, and has different names (for example Brand Box Model), making its origin not entirely clear. At Unilever, they use the model in the form presented in this appendix. The model involves eight steps/stages that can lead to differentiating and relevant brand positioning (see Figure A.1): (1) competitive environment, (2) target, (3) consumer insight, (4) benefits, (5) values and personality, (6) reasons to believe, (7) discriminator, and (8) brand essence. The Brand Key Model is all about taking stock of all relevant information for these eight subjects, by putting some succinct points to paper for each (in total about one A4 sheet). In doing so, you can make a distinction between describing the current situation ('ist', which is referred to as the master key in this model) and a separate description of the future, desired situation ('soll'; in this model the vision key). At Unilever a separate brand key is completed for each extension. In the following we will further explain the eight stages of the Brand Key Model, including indications of the model's shortcomings, and finally present another model that was derived from this one.

The Brand Key Model works on the assumption that a brand manager takes the following eight steps in a brand positioning process (see Figure A.1, facing page).

1 Competitive environment: the first step on the road to clear positioning involves mapping the competition situation. This means taking stock of the brands/products that a customer can consider when making his or her

> The market and alternative choices as seen by the consumer and the relative value the brand offers in that market.

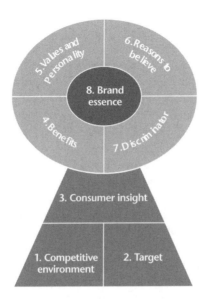

FIGURE A.1 The eight stages of the Brand Key

purchase decision. These can include direct competitors – in the sense that Pepsi-Cola is a 'real' competitor of Coca-Cola – but also less obvious competitors that, for example, tailor to the generic need for the quenching of thirst. At this stage, the brand manager will not only have to identify competing brands, but also consider how these position themselves in the market, and which associations customers/consumers have with these brands. A handy aid for the taking stock of competitors is Porter's Five Forces Model (see Section 5.1).

2 Target: this step consists of identifying the (desired) target group, not only in terms of demographics, but also in terms of attitudes and values. This, in principle, means answering the question why the brand in question makes the best choice for a certain person and/or in a certain situation.

> The person and situation for which the brand is always the best choice, defined in terms of their attitudes and values; not just demographics.

3 Consumer insight: for a brand to be successful in a market, it will have to tie in with a relevant consumer insight.

A consumer insight concerns a latent purchase motive in the target group with relation to the product. A consumer insight does not merely answer the question why consumers buy a certain product, but rather lays bare the latent needs driving consumers to buy a certain product. This is not just about finding out why consumers buy a certain product, but also about finding out why they would *not* buy it. By way of example, we can refer to the

> That element of all you know about the target consumer and their needs (in this competitive environment upon which the brand is founded).

consumer insight behind the Coca-Cola Zero launch. Research had shown that men found Coca-Cola Light too feminine. The Coca-Cola Company countered that by launching Coca-Cola Zero, a more manly looking soft drink, which did tie in with a more male experience framework in terms of name and of look and feel. The significant insight here was the reason why men would *not* buy Coca-Cola Light; Coca-Cola Zero was, eventually, based on that insight. The description of relevant insights for a brand can sometimes overlap with the target group description (in particular when it concerns values and attitudes).

> Coca-Cola Zero is intended for men who are looking for exquisite taste, but without the sugar. Coca-Cola is looking to appeal to men with a carefree lifestyle with all that entails, who do not want to settle for possible downsides (no compromising on taste). The Zero message is therefore 'Great life without downsides'. In order to make this message hit home with the target group, Coca-Cola looked into their passions. In the Netherlands, racing and gaming were identified as their passions. On the basis of these drivers, Coca-Cola subsequently set up targeted marketing communication campaigns for the Zero target group.

4   Benefits: where steps 1–3 were outward-looking (competition, target group and consumer insights), step 4 is the first of a series of more inward-looking steps with a focus on the brand itself. This

> The differing functional and emotional benefits that motivate purchase.

stage involves identifying the benefits offered by the brand. These benefits can be both of a functional nature (for example, emphasizing the presence of certain ingredients in a margarine brand) and of a psycho-social nature (by margarine appealing to the value of motherly care).

5   Values and personality: the central question in this phase is what values a brand has to appeal to (what does the brand stand for and what does it believe in?). Brands appealing to values are supposed to click with the consumer. This means not only better *brand recognition*, but also a greater degree of *appreciation* by the consumer. Well-known value systems are Mitchell's VALS typology and Rokeach's RVS typology (see p. 85). When designating values, two aspects arise: (a) values should not be communicated directly, but should in the end still resound in the advertising message; (b) values generally do not make reference to the points on which a brand differentiates itself. Where the latter is concerned, it should be noted that the difference between brands lies mainly in the question of how values are converted into practical consequences. Values can also be personified, describing the brand in terms of personal(ity) characteristics or traits. A way of doing this in marketing communication is using celebrities with these characteristics in advertising (such as George Clooney in the Nespresso ads).

> The brand values – what the brand stands for and believes in and/or its personality.

6   Reason to believe: at this stage of the process, the idea is to formulate arguments based on which the target group will believe the brand is the best option for them. This preference can mostly be captured in sentences such as 'I buy brand X *because* . . .'. These arguments can be used in advertising, but actual customer contacts can also be set up in such a way that they 'prove' to consumers that the brand actually stands for what it claims to stand for. For example, a travel agency claiming to be very cheap will support that image better by having austere decorations than with lots of luxury and sleek style in their agency interiors. One example is the case of a certain scientific search engine building a delay into the programme, because users had little confidence in its accuracy owing to the rapid return of search results.

> The proof we offer to substantiate the positioning.

7 Discriminator: in this penultimate step the brand manager will have to state concisely what the actual difference is between the brand in question and other brands. This difference can mostly be captured in sentences such as '*Only* brand X has . . .'.

> Single most compelling and competitive statement the target consumer would make for buying the brand.

8 The brand essence: this is a summary of stages 4–7. The idea here is to catch the brand's essence in one or two words, such as 'driving enjoyment' for BMW.

> The distillation of the brand's genetic code into one clear thought.

In a later version of this model, marketing staff at Unilever added one more step in the form of the brand's root strengths. This stage involves pinpointing what has made the brand what it is, what it can build on. Describing root strengths should be done before the above eight steps.

The advantage of the Brand Key Model is that it profiles virtually every single relevant step in a positioning process; but the downside is that it overemphasizes the outside-in approach, making the model less suitable for brands where the inside-out approach is relevant (such as in the case of service providers). The outside-in emphasis particularly comes to the fore in the fact that 'values and personality' feature rather late on in the model (stage 5). When positioning a brand that depends strongly on an inside-out movement, values and personality tend to serve as the basic principle of positioning: it is therefore rather tricky to apply this model for service providers, for example.

Note

1 Source: www.eurib.org (online resource centre – subject: Positioning).

APPENDIX B

Comprehensive list of values[1]

Terminal values

- Adult partner relation, adult love, mature love
- (True) friendship, close friendship, companionship, solidarity
- Freedom, freedom of choice, carefreeness, independence
- Equality, anti-status, justice, fraternity
- Accomplishment, self-development, career, being successful
- Power, leadership, leading role
- Status, social standing, prestige, being admired, good social position
- Knowledge, general development, mental development
- Individuality, personality, being different, unique lifestyle
- Life of luxury, comfortable life, wealth
- Thrilling life, adventurous life, active life, exciting life
- Enjoyment (of life), joie de vivre, cosiness, fun
- Social recognition, social acceptance, being appreciated by others
- Wisdom, maturity, adulthood, sensibility
- Inner harmony, being at ease, peace and quiet, relaxedness, anti-stress, satisfaction
- Health, vitality, vigour
- (Physical) attractiveness, looking good, being handsome/pretty, sex appeal
- Self-respect, sense of self-worth, self-confidence, self-esteem, sense of achievement
- Youth, youthfulness
- Sense of place, sense of belonging, having your own home
- Frugality, thrift
- Personal security, close-knit family ties, family security
- Having offspring, starting a family

- Safety, living in a safe world, safety for family and friends, being spared loss, fear, pain and unhappiness
- Security, being able to count on something/someone
- Keeping everything the way it is
- Taking time to yourself, looking after yourself
- Romance, being in love, love
- Eroticism, sex, seduction, sensuality
- Love for children
- Care for others
- Better environment, love of nature
- Being able to stay true to yourself
- Happiness, satisfaction, frame of mind where all wishes are fulfilled and in which one is satisfied with the current situation on all fronts
- Aesthetics, beauty of nature, beauty of art
- Sense of belonging
- Better quality of life (working to live)
- High standard of living (living to work)
- National freedom
- Salvation
- Enjoying the simple things in life
- Self-knowledge, knowing yourself
- Striving for a better world
- Nice living environment
- A world at peace (free of war and conflict)
- National security
- Achieving something (in life), talented, competence
- (Personal) satisfaction
- Social harmony
- Patriotism
- Acting like an adult, maturity

Instrumental values (personality traits)

- Ambitious, hard-working
- Cheerful, upbeat
- Open-minded, broad-minded views, unprejudiced
- Tidiness, decent, orderly, neat
- Courageous, standing for something, standing up for your opinion
- Forgiving
- Helpful, ready to help

- Honest, sincere
- Creative, imaginative
- Being able to take care of yourself, self-reliance, independence
- Intelligence, intellectual, education, sensible
- Logical reasoning, logical, rational, consistent
- Affection, tenderness, loving
- Sense of duty, obedient, responsible
- Respect, respectful towards others
- Well-mannered, politeness
- Reliability, responsible
- (Self-)discipline, (self-)control, disciplined
- Competent, capable
- Independence
- Dutifulness
- Accomplishment, completion, fulfilment
- Being up-to-date, moving with the times
- Self-confidence, self-assured, independent
- Composure, controlled, calmness
- Collaboration
- Expedient, purposeful, efficient, time-saving, quick
- Mobility
- Good morals
- Care, upbringing
- Optimism
- Emotional, passion
- Peaceful, peace-loving, peaceable
- Popularity
- Practical (attitude)
- Quality
- Relaxation, winding down
- Simplicity, uncomplicated
- Spontaneity
- Tradition
- Variety
- Vitality
- Being successful
- Excite, excited
- Adventurous
- Enjoying, enjoyment, delight, pleasure, fun
- Tolerant

- Humour
- Sympathy (compassion)
- Innovate, innovating
- Intimacy, bond
- Friendliness
- Loyalty, loyal
- Materialism, having a lot of money
- Originality, original
- Stylish, elegant
- Convenience
- Distinguished (standing out for your manners and appearance)
- Groundbreaking
- Challenge(s)
- Modest(y)
- Ability to adapt, flexible
- Integrity
- Unique, distinguishing
- Emancipation
- Femininity
- Masculinity
- (Appreciation, love of) art
- (Appreciation, love of) culture
- (Appreciation, love of) literature

Note

1 Source: Samenvatting waardelijsten [Summarized value lists] by Van de Pol and Laskaris (1994), quoted in Franzen *et al.* (1998, pp. 100–103).

BIBLIOGRAPHY

Aaker, D.A. (1991) *Managing Brand Equity: Capitalizing on the Value of a Brand Name*. The Free Press, New York.
Aaker, D.A. (1996) *Building Strong Brands*. The Free Press, New York.
Abrahams, J. (1999) *The Mission Statement Book (301 Corporate Mission Statements from America's Top Companies)*. Ten Speed Press, Berkeley.
Alba, J.W., Hutchinson, J.W., Lynch J.G. Jr (1991) Memory and decision making. In: H.H. Kassarjian and T.S. Robertson (eds). *Handbook of Consumer Research*. Prentice Hall, New York, pp. 1–49.
Batey, M. (2008) *Brand Meaning*. Routledge, New York.
Brewer, W.F., Treyens, J.C. (1981) Role of schemata in memory for places. *Cognitive Psychology*, vol. 13, pp. 207–230.
Brown, T.J., Dacin, P. A. (1997) The company and the product: corporate associations and consumer product responses. *Journal of Marketing*, vol. 61, no. 1, pp. 68–84.
Cameron, K.S., Quinn, R.E. (2006) *Diagnosing and Changing Organizational Culture: Based on the Competing Values Framework*, revised edition. Jossey Bass, San Francisco.
Carpenter, G.S., Glazer, R., Nakamoto, K. (1994) Meaningful brands from meaningless differentiation: the dependence on irrelevant attributes. *Journal of Marketing Research*, vol. 31, no. 3, pp. 339–350.
Collins, J.C, Porras, J.I. (1997) *Built to Last: Successful Habits of Visionary Companies*. Harper Business, New York.
Coppenhagen, R. (2002) *Creatieregie: visie and verbinding bij verandering*. Scriptum Management, Schiedam, Netherlands.
Davidson, J.H. (1987) *Offensive Marketing or, How to Make Your Competitors Followers*. Penguin, Harmondsworth, UK.
DelVecchio, D. (2000) Moving beyond fit: the role of brand portfolio characteristics in consumer evaluations of brand reliability. *Journal of Product and Brand Management*, vol. 9, no. 7, pp. 457–471.
Farquhar, H., Herr, P.M. (1993) The dual structure of brand associations. In: D.A. Aaker and A.L. Biel (eds). *Brand Equity and Advertising: Advertising's Role in Building Strong Brands*. Lawrence Erlbaum, Hillsdale, USA, pp. 263–276.

Franzen, G., Goessens, C., Hoogerbrugge, M., Kappert, C., Schuring, R.J., Vogel, M. (1998) *Merken and reclame: hoe reclame-effectiviteit brand equity beïnvloedt*. Kluwer Bedrijfsinformatie, Deventer, Netherlands.

Freiberg, K., Freiberg, J. (1997) *Nuts! Southwest Airlines' Crazy Recipe for Business and Personal Success*. Broadway Books, New York.

Green, P.E., Carmone, F.J., Smith, S.M. (1989) *Multidimensional Scaling: Concepts and Applications*. Allyn and Bacon, Boston.

Gürhan-Canli, Z., Maheswaran, D. (1998) The effects of extensions on brand name dilution and enhancement. *Journal of Marketing Research*, vol. 35, no. 4, pp. 464–473.

Gutman, J. (1982) A means–end chain model based on consumer categorization processes. *Journal of Marketing*, vol. 46, Spring, pp. 60–72.

Henderson, P.W., Cote, J.A. (1998) Guidelines for selecting or modifying logos. *Journal of Marketing*, vol. 62, no. 2, pp. 14–30.

Ind, N. (1997) *The Corporate Brand*. Macmillan Press, London, UK.

Hofstede, G., Hofstede, G.J. (2004) *Culture and Organizations; Software of the Mind*. McGraw-Hill, New York.

Hooley, G., Piercy, N.F., Nicoulaud, B. (2008) *Marketing Strategy and Competitive Positioning*. Pearson Education, Harlow, UK.

Kapferer, J.N. (2001) *(Re)inventing The Brand: Can Top Brands Survive the New Market Realities?* Kogan Page, London, UK.

Kapferer, J.N. (2008) *The New Strategic Brand Management: Creating and Sustaining Brand Equity Long Term*. Kogan Page, London, UK.

Keller, K.L. (2001) Building customer based brand equity: a blueprint for creating strong brands. Working paper. Report no. 01-107, Marketing Science Institute, Cambridge.

Keller, K.L. (2008) *Strategic Brand Management: Building, Measuring, and Managing Brand Equity*. Pearson Higher Education, Upper Saddle River.

Keller, K.L., Apéria, T., Georgson, M. (2008) *Strategic Brand Management: A European Perspective*. Prentice Hall, Harlow, UK.

Kim, W.C., Mauborgne, R. (2005) *Blue Ocean Strategy: How to Create Uncontested Market Space and Make the Competition Irrelevant*. Harvard Business School Press, Boston.

King, S. (1991) Brand building in the 1990s. *Journal of Marketing Management*, vol. 7, no. 1, pp. 3–13.

Knox, S. (2004) Positioning and branding your organisation. *Journal of Product and Brand Management*, vol. 13, no. 2, pp. 105–115.

Kralingen, R. van (1999) *Superbrands: merken en markten van morgen*. Samsom, Deventer, Netherlands.

Krishnan, H.S. (1996) Characteristics of memory associations: a consumer-based brand equity perspective. *International Journal of Research in Marketing*, vol. 13, no. 4, pp. 389–405.

Laforet, S., Saunders, J. (1994) Managing brand portfolios: how the leaders do it. *Journal of Advertising Research*, vol. 34, no. 5, pp. 64–76.

Laforet, S., Saunders, J. (1999) Managing brand portfolios: why leaders do what they do. *Journal of Advertising Research*, vol. 39, no. 1, pp. 51–66.

Laforet, S., Saunders, J. (2005) Managing brand portfolios: how strategies have changed. *Journal of Advertising Research*, vol. 45, no. 3, pp. 314–327.

Loken, B. (2006) Consumer psychology: categorization, inferences, affect, and persuasion. *Annual Review of Psychology*, vol. 57, pp. 453–485.

McClure, M., Li, J., Tomlin, D., Cypert, K.S., Montague, L.M., Montague, P.R. (2004) Neural correlates of behavioral preference for culturally familiar drinks. *Neuron*, vol. 44, pp. 379–387.

Myers, J.H. (1996) *Segmentation and Positioning for Strategic Marketing Decisions*. South-Western Educational Publishers, Cincinnati.

Milberg, S.J., Park, C.W., McCarthy, M.S. (1997) Managing negative feedback effects associated with brand extensions: the impact of alternative branding strategies. *Journal of Consumer Psychology*, vol. 6, no. 2, pp. 119–140.

Miller, S., Berry, L. (1998) Brand salience versus brand image: two theories of advertising effectiveness. *Journal of Advertising Research*, vol. 38, no. 5, pp. 77–82.

Olson, J.C., Reynolds, T.J. (1983) Understanding consumers' cognitive structures: implications for advertising strategy. In: L. Percy and A. Woodside (eds). *Advertising and Consumer Psychology*. Lexington Books, Lexington, pp. 77–90.

Porter, M.E. (1998) *Competitive strategy: Techniques for Analyzing Industries and Competitors*. The Free Press, New York.

Reynolds, T.J., Craddock, A.B. (2001) The application of the MECCAS model to the development and assessment of advertising strategy: a case study. In: T.J. Reynolds and J.C. Olson (eds). *Understanding Consumer Decision Making: The Means–End Approach to Marketing and Advertising Strategy*. Lawrence Erlbaum, Mahwah, pp. 163–182.

Reynolds, T.J., Gutman, J. (1984) Laddering: extending the repertory grid methodology to construct attribute–consequence–value hierarchies. In: R.E. Pitts Jr and A.G. Woodside (eds). *Personal Values and Consumer Psychology*. Lexington Books, Lexington, pp. 155–167.

Reynolds, T.J., Gutman, J. (2001) Laddering theory, method, analysis, and interpretation. In: T.J. Reynolds and J.C. Olson (eds). *Understanding Consumer Decision Making: The Means–End Approach to Marketing and Advertising Strategy*. Lawrence Erlbaum, Mahwah, pp. 25–62.

Ries, A., Trout, J. (1986) *Positioning: The Battle for Your Mind*, revised edition. Warner Books, New York.

Ries, A., Trout, J. (2001) *Positioning: The Battle for Your Mind – 20th Anniversary Edition*. McGraw-Hill, New York.

Ries, A., Trout, J. (2006) *Marketing Warfare*. McGraw-Hill, New York.

Riezebos, R. (2003) *Brand Management: A Theoretical and Practical Approach*. Financial Times/Prentice Hall, Harlow, UK.

Riezebos, R. (2007) Innocent: little tasty drinks, enjoy! In: A. Pappers and M Schäffer (eds). *Coolbrands, The Guru Book*. Cool Unlimited, Amsterdam, The Netherlands, pp. 166–169.

Riezebos, J., Riezebos, R. (2004) *Verzamelde merken: de betekenis van 3166 namen van producten en bedrijven verklaard.* Sdu Uitgevers, The Hague, The Netherlands.

Roedder John, D., Loken, B., Joiner, C. (1998) The negative impact of extensions: Can flagship products be diluted? *Journal of Marketing*, vol. 62, no. 1, pp. 19–32.

Rokeach, M. (1973) *The Nature of Human Values.* The Free Press, New York.

Rossiter, J.R., Bellman, S. (2005) *Marketing Communications: Theory and Applications.* Pearson Education, Frenchs Forest, Australia.

Rossiter, J.R., Percy, L. (1997) *Advertising Communications and Promotion Management.* McGraw-Hill, New York.

Rossiter, J.R., Percy, L. (2001) The a–b–e model of benefit focus in advertising. In: T.J. Reynolds and J.C. Olson (eds). *Understanding Consumer Decision Making: The Means–End Approach to Marketing and Advertising Strategy.* Lawrence Erlbaum, Mahwah, pp. 183–213.

Roth, M.S. (1992) Depth versus breadth strategies for global brand image management. *Journal of Advertising*, vol. 21, no. 2, pp. 25–36.

Sengupta, S. (2005) *Brand Positioning: Strategies for Competitive Advantage.* Tata McGraw-Hill, Delhi, India.

Simonin, B.L., Ruth, J.A. (1998) Is a company known by the company it keeps? Assessing the spillover effects of brand alliances on consumer brand attitudes. *Journal of Marketing Research*, vol. 35, no. 1, pp. 30–42.

Sujan, M., Bettman, J.R. (1989) The effects of brand positioning strategies on consumers' brand category perceptions: some insights from schema research. *Journal of Marketing Research*, vol. 26, no. 4, pp. 454–467.

Sullivan, M. (1990) Measuring image spillovers in umbrella-branded products. *Journal of Business*, vol. 63, no. 3, pp. 309–329.

Tybout, A.M., Calder. B.J., Sternthal, B. (1981) Using information processing theory to design marketing strategies. *Journal of Marketing Research*, vol. 18, no. 1, pp. 73–79.

Van Lee, R., Fabish, L., McGaw, N. (2005) The value of corporate values. *Strategy + Business*, issue 39, pp. 1–14.

Velden, J. van der (2007) *Océ: van nature innovatief, 1877–2007.* Lecturis, Eindhoven.

Wansink, B. (2003) Using laddering to understand and leverage a brand's equity. *Qualitative Market Research: An International Journal*, vol. 6, no. 2, pp. 111–118.

Wit, B. de, Meyer, R. (2005) *Strategy Synthesis: Resolving Strategy Paradoxes to Create Competitive Advantage.* Thomson, London, UK.

INDEX

Accor group 118
accountability 4, 42
active brand awareness 154–6
adhocracy 44
advertising 5, 38, 42, 84–5, 142, 156, 161–5; *see also* marketing
Alfa Bier 109
Alfa Romeo 83–5
Apple 101–2
architecture, brand 14–15, 18–19, 51–74
argumentation 148–9
Asia 55
assisted brand awareness 153
associations
    brand name strategy 58
    choices 12–13
    evoking brand 156–65
    means–end chains 90–1, 93–5, 97, 129, 137–8
    mind management 76, 80–7, 128
    propositions of products 62
    target groups 2, 8–9
attributes
    choosing 139–47
    external analysis 127–8
    laddering 92–4
    means–end chains 137–8
    mind management 76, 80–7
    values 89–91, 97
authenticity 5–6, 146, 149
Axe deodorant 108

baby wipes 145
balanced brand portfolios 59–68
banks 58
batteries 145
Ben & Jerry's 109
BMW 78–9, 112, 141–2
Bonne Maman 5–6
bottom-up questioning 92–3
BPM *see* Brand Portfolio Model
BPS *see* Brand Positioning Sheets
Bradham, Caleb 10
Brand Key Model 167–72
Brand Portfolio Model (BPM) 65–6
Brand Positioning Sheets (BPS) 133, 137, 147–51
brand-driven approaches 6–9
brand-product class connections 77–82
Brand–Target Group–Competitors (BTC) model 13–15, 19, 51, 75, 99–100, 135
brand-values connection 85–7
broad brands 62
BTC *see* Brand–Target Group–Competitors model
b-to-b *see* business-to-business approaches
Budweiser 76
business orientation 20, 23–30
business-to-business approaches (b-to-b) 118–21
buyers 101

call centers 117
Cameron, K.S. 42
car brands 101, 151
car navigation systems 104–5

car safety 12–13, 87
carve-out operations 59–65
categorization 77–82, 94, 97, 136, 141, 154
C-B-M-V model *see* Characteristics, Benefits, Meanings, Values
celebrity chefs 6–7
Characteristics, Benefits, Meanings, Values (C-B-M-V model) 142–3
checklists 71–4, 127–31
checkout queues 94
cigarette advertising 142
Cillit Bang 111
cleaning products 111
closed business-orientations 23–4, 39, 49
cluster brands 161–2
co-branding 166
Coca-Cola 9–11, 68–9
coffee 163
cognitive maps 102
communication 35, 82, 89–90, 142–3, 156–65
communicative realization 151–65
comparative advertising 163
competencies 20, 24–6, 30–6, 104
competition
  BPS 148
  BTC model 13–15
  Coca-Cola and Pepsi-Cola 10–11
  core competencies 31
  corporate identity 18, 25–7
  differentiation 2, 8, 141–2
  points of difference 12
  repositioning 136
competitive value model 42–4
competitor analysis 99–131
concrete customer contacts 89–90, 97
Connected Thinking 120
consequences 139–48
consistency 84–5, 166
contents
  associations 83–4
  brand portfolios 59, 63–4
control business-orientations 23–4, 39, 49
cooking-related products 6–7
core competencies 20, 30–6, 104
core products 66–7, 152

corporate
  culture, types of 42
  brands 4, 58, 69–70
  identity 13–14, 18–50, 71–3
  mentality 109
  positioning approaches 103–4
  product brands contrast 19, 53–7
  values 21, 46–9
corporate ability
  brand architecture 63–4
  business-to-business 118–21
  checklist 131
  durable consumer goods 113
  FMCGs 109–11
  non-profit organizations 122–3
  organization-based 104
  product-based 104
  services 116
costs 5, 33–4, 59, 63–4
creative guidelines 161–5
crisp brands 91
CRM *see* customer relationship management
culture 21, 41–6, 117
Cuprinol 109
customer
  contacts 35, 89–90, 93–4, 97
  focus 26–7
  service 114–15
  values 21, 46–9
customer relationship management (CRM) 118

DAF Trucks 120–1
dance events 34
Dekkers, Marlies 40
Dell 101, 108
design-based positioning
  business-to-business 119–21
  checklist 131
  FMCGs 110–11
  market-variable-based 106
  non-profit organizations 123–4
  services 116–17
design expertise 33
differentiation
  choosing market positions 139–42, 148
  competition 2, 8, 102–8, 136

core competencies 31
corporate values 48
introduction 5, 9
MAYA principle 81
product brand names 55
R&D 33
digital services 22–3
direct questions 93
display items 135, 151
distance between products 62–5
distribution-based positioning
  business-to-business 119–21
  checklist 131
  FMCGs 110
  market-variable-based 106
  non-profit organizations 123–4
  services 116–18
Double A Paper 121
DSM 120
dual positioning 108
Dubai 122
durable consumer goods 112–14

e-cards sector 118
economic risks 158
emotional benefits
  business-to-business 119–21
  checklist 131
  FMCGs 110–11
  non-profit organizations 123, 125
  receiver-based 108
  services 116
employee-based approaches
  business-to-business 119
  checklist 131
  durable consumer goods 112
  FMCGs 110
  non-profit organizations 122–3
  positioning approaches 103–4
  services 114–16
employees
  behaviour 16
  core competencies 32
  corporate and customer values 48
  culture 41–5
  motivation 35–6, 43–4
  organization-oriented organizations 28–9
endorsement 53–4, 58

entrepreneurs 44, 137
essence, brand 149–50
excellence 26, 44
exclusive sales arguments 80
expertise 32–3
extension products 153, 165
external analysis 75–131
external competition 100–1
external environments 15, 135
external logistics 32, 34–5

fabric-cleaning products 159
family culture 42–3
fashion design 40
fast-moving consumer goods 93, 110–12, 142
feature positioning 122
FedEx 121
financial aspects 54, 59, 63–4, 88–9, 158
Five Forces Model 100–2
flagship products 63–4, 68–9, 146
flexible business-orientations 39, 49
FMCG *see* fast-moving consumer goods
formal culture 43
fruit juices 81–2
functional hierarchies 43
fundamental needs 85–6
future vision 36–41

Gibson guitars 112
goods and services 3, 6–7
Google 32, 38, 117, 121
grocery store chains 35
grounding 31
GSUS 112
Gutman, Jonathan 89

Harley-Davidson 63
Harrods 115, 135–7, 151
Heijn, Albert 35
Hertog Jan beer 109
heuristics 78
hierarchical setups 43
history of organizations 20–3
HRM *see* human resources management
Huggies 143–4
human resource management (HRM) 21, 88
human rights 125

ice cream 109
iconic brands 155
ID&T 33–4
identity
  brand 10, 12, 135, 148
  corporate 13–14, 18–50, 71–3
  repositioning 137
image 12, 54, 63–4, 151–2
immaterial ratios 114–15
individualistic motivations 160
information brands 163
Innocent Drinks 81–2, 145–7, 150–1
innovation 32–3, 41, 44–5, 134, 149
instrumental values 86, 174–6
Intel 101
interactive consumption 114–15
internal analysis 18–70
internal competition 100–1
internal environments 13–15, 134–5
internal logistics 32–4
Internet 5, 100
interpersonal contacts 41
Interpolis 36
interviews 92–6, 128–9
involvement 157–8, 161–5
I organizations 24
It organizations 26

Jaguar 101
Jamie Oliver 6–7
jeans 164–5

Kamen, Nick 164–5
Kelly's repertory grid method 92
Kerry, John 164
KLM Airlines 44

labour markets 4, 88–9
laddering 90, 92–6
leadership 40, 43–4
level 139, 142–7
Levi 164–5
licence to operate 88–9
Loewry, Raymond 81
logos 8, 82, 56–7, 155
luxury brands 145
Lynx deodorant 108

McKinsey & Company 120
management buyouts 134
marketing 19–20, 24, 26, 85–6, 88–9, 137, 153; *see also* advertising
marketing-variable-based approaches
  business-to-business 119–21, 131
  competitor analysis 106–7
  consumer goods 110–14
  non-profit organizations 123–5
  services 115–18
market-oriented organizations 24, 26–8, 30, 32, 39, 43, 49
markets
  choosing a position 133–66
  competitor analysis 99–131
  core competencies 35
  means–end chains 91–2
  segmentation 65–7
  soft drinks 11
  vision 36–7
marlies dekkers 40
matching products 152
material/immaterial ratios 114–15
MAYA *see* 'most advanced yet acceptable' principle
meanings 95–6, 139–48
means–end chain analysis 76, 87–96, 128–30, 137–40, 143–4, 148
media explosion 1, 4–5, 66
media fragmentation 59
memory nodes 76–7, 80–1
mental associations 97, 141, 165–6
mental environments 127–8
mentality
  business-to-business 118–21
  checklist 131
  consumer goods 110, 112
  corporate 109
  non-profit organizations 122
  organization-based 104
  services 114–16
mergers 133–5
metal packaging 120
mind management 76–87
mind shares 11–12, 76
mission 36–41, 56–7
Mona brand 59–60, 64, 134
Montague, Read 11

'most advanced yet acceptable' (MAYA) principle 81
motivations 32, 35–6, 43–4, 61–2, 157–9
motorcycles 78–9
mythical brands 164–5

name, brand 52–8, 165
name awareness
  business-to-business 119–21
  checklist 131
  FMCGs 110–11
  marketing-variable-based 107
  non-profit organizations 123–4
  services 116, 118
nappies 143–4
narrow brands 62
natural grouping 92
negative motivations 157–61, 163
Nestlé 53, 56, 120–1
new products 134, 156, 165–6
Nike 149
Nivea 69
no-go areas 153
non-profit organizations 121–5

observable names 8
Océ 21–3, 41, 45, 121
Office Christmas 121
offsetting 141
OMO brand 159
OPCOs *see* operating companies
open business-orientations 39, 49
operating companies (OPCOs) 21
operational excellence 26
organization-based approaches
  business-to-business 118–21
  checklist 131
  consumer goods 109–10, 113
  product-based 104–5
  services 114–15
organization-oriented organizations 24, 28–9, 32, 35–6, 39, 49
organizations 1, 3–4, 16, 53–4, 88–9
outside-in approaches 16
outsourcing 26

packaging 106
Pampers 143–4

passively known awareness 154
Pemberton, John 10
Pepsi-Cola 9–11, 79
perceptions 61–2, 78–9, 83, 134, 153, 158
performance culture 43–4
personal needs 85–6
personality traits 174–6
petrol 159–6
Philips 53–4
pigeonholing 82
points of difference (PODs) 12, 70–81, 127, 140–1
points of parity (POPs) 12, 80–1, 127, 140–1
politics 164
POPs *see* points of parity
Porsche 165–6
portable music players 101–2
portfolios, brand 52, 56, 59–68
positive motivations 157–61, 163–5
postal companies 33–4
potential competition 100–2
premium brands 66
prices
  authenticity 146
  brand portfolios 65–8
  checklist 131
  competitor analysis 93, 106, 110–11, 116, 118–19, 123–4
  consumer involvement 158
  petrol 160
  positioning approaches 103
  propositions 61–2
PricewaterhouseCoopers (PWC) 120
printing companies 121
problem-preventing approaches 145
process-oriented organizations 24, 26, 39, 49
product-based approaches
  approaches 103
  business-to-business 118–21
  checklist 131
  durable consumer goods 112–14
  FMCGs 109–10
  non-profit organizations 122–3
  product-based 104–5
  services 116–17
product-driven approaches 6–9

Index

product-oriented organizations 24–5, 30, 32, 38–9, 42, 49
products
  attributes meaning 89
  benefits 83, 142
  brand contrast 6–9
  brands 19, 46, 53–7, 59–69
  categorization 94
  choosing 151–3
  class 76–7, 80, 91, 95–7, 139–41, 155
  explosion 1, 3
  features 83, 94–5, 105, 110, 116, 118–21, 123, 131
  names 58
projects 44
prominent brands 154
propositions 60–2, 68–70
prototypical approaches
  approaches 103
  business-to-business 118–21
  checklist 131
  consumer goods 109–10, 112–14
  differentiation 140
  non-profit organizations 122–3
  product-based 104–5
  services 116–17
psycho-social risks 158
Pura 159–6
purchasing approaches 61–2, 120, 157–9, 161–4
PWC *see* PricewaterhouseCoopers

qualitative assessment 137
quality of products 2–3
questioning 92–3

R&D *see* research and development
ranking companies 4
rational benefit approaches 103, 105, 110, 116, 118–21, 123, 131
rationalization of brand portfolios 66–7
recall 156
recategorization 165–6
receiver-based approaches
  business-to-business 119
  checklist 131
  consumer goods 110–11, 131
  non-profit organizations 123, 125

positioning 107–8
services 116, 118
recognized brands 155
relevance 31, 93–4, 137, 148
repositioning 133–7, 165–6
research and development (R&D) 21, 26–7, 33
retail services 114–18
Reynolds, Thomas J. 89
risk perceptions 158
Rockwool 58
Rokeach Value Survey (RVS) 86

safety 12–13, 85, 87, 108
Salanova 24–5
sales and marketing 137
SCA *see* sustainable competitive advantage
schema, brand 76–7, 87, 95–6
Schipol Airport, Amsterdam 104
Schultz, Howard 37–9
search engines 32, 38, 117
secondary school student choices 94–6, 138–9
self-fulfilment 138–9
self-knowledge 16
Sensation White 34
service-providing operations 44–5
services 3, 105, 114–18
shareholder power 4
Shell 58, 159–6
signs 8–9
situation approaches
  business-to-business 119–21
  checklist 131
  FMCGs 110
  non-profit organizations 123, 125
  receiver-based 107–8
  services 116
smoothies 81–2, 145–7, 150–1
Snack-a-Jacks 105
social aspects 48, 85–6, 138–9
soft drinks 10–11
Sony 101
Southwest Airlines 28–9, 104
Starbucks 28, 37–8
statements 150
stereotypical categorization 82

strategic level
    brand portfolios 59
    management 21, 28, 41, 48
    product portfolios 63–4
strong brands 59, 61–2, 85, 87
sub-branding 52, 68–9
substitutes 102
sub-target groups 89
super brands 9
supermarkets 33
suppliers 101
sustainability 47
sustainable competitive advantage (SCA) 31–2
swiftboating 164
symbolism 56–7, 108

target groups
    analysis 75–97
    brands 2, 8–9, 58, 68, 163
    BTC model 13–16
    business-to-business 119–21
    checklist 131
    competitors 99–100
    consistency 166
    corporate and customer values 47
    corporate identity 18
    FMCGs 110–11
    market positions 148, 150
    means–end chains 138
    non-profit organizations 123, 125
    perceptions 134
    positioning approaches 103, 107–8
    product *versus* corporate brands 54
    propositions of products 62
    repositioning 136
    selection of 148
    services 116
    sub-branding 69–70
targeted positioning 2, 13, 135
telecommunications 100, 165
television 4–5
terminal values 85–6, 173–4
territory brands 163–4
Tesco 117
The Brand Circle 152–3
They organizations 26
TNT 33–4, 48
toilet paper 144–5

TOMA *see* top-of-mind awareness
TomTom 104–5
top-down questioning 92–3
top-of-mind awareness (TOMA) 154
transparency 47
truck manufacturers 120–1
trust 36
trusted brands 155

unawareness 154
uncola strategy 141
Unilever 44, 56–7, 65–7, 159
unique selling propositions (USPs) 80
universities 94–6, 138–9, 158
UPC 35
USPs *see* unique selling propositions

value-based positioning
    business-to-business 119–21
    checklist 131
    FMCGs 110
    non-profit organizations 123, 125
    receiver-based 108
    services 116
values
    attributes 89–91, 97
    brand 46–7, 85–7, 148
    choosing 139–47
    corporate and customer 21, 46–9
    laddering 92–4
    list of 173–6
    means–end chains 137–8
    mind management 76
van der Grinten, Lodewyk 22–3, 45
Vanish 111
vertical integration 101
Vietnam veterans 164
Vifit 59–60, 64, 134
Virgin 27, 104, 115
vision and mission 20, 36–41
visual brand identity 165
vitality mission 56–7

weak brands 87
well-considered choices 12
window displays 135, 151
woodcare sector 109

yoghurt products 59–60, 64–5

BRAND NAME INDEX

Absolut Vodka 106, 110–11
Accenture 134
Accor group 115–17
Acrobat software 102
Actimel 65
Adobe 102
After Eight 2, 108
Aibo 55
Air France-KLM 44
Albert Heijn 35
Aldi 33, 106
Alessi 113–14, 166
Alfa Bier 109–10
Alfa Romeo 8, 83–5
Always 20, 55
Amnesty International 122–3, 125
Andersen Consulting 134
Apple 30–1, 33, 102, 106, 134, 151
Aquarel 121
Armani 145
Arthur Andersen 134
Atari 82
Audi 15
Avia 154
Axe 55, 108

Baby-Dry 143–4
Bacardi 108, 111
Bang & Olufsen 53, 106
Barnes & Noble 28
Becel 67
Ben & Jerry's 104, 109–10
Benckiser 4
Bentley 101

Bilbao 123–4
B-Live 108, 110
Blue Band 67
BMW 3, 66, 101, 112, 141–2, 171
BMW C1 78–9, 141
Bolton Group 55, 109
Bonne Maman 5–6
Bora 69
Bosch 101, 119–21
BP 154
Bravia 55
British Airways 53
British Army 122–3
British Rail 155
British Steel 133–4
Budweiser 76

C&A 61–2
Calvin Klein 145
Camcorder 55
Camel 142
Caterpillar 153
Cayenne 166
Cillit Bang 111, 161
Citroën 33
Club Med 116
Clute, Texas 2
Coca-Cola 9–11, 69, 76, 169
Coca-Cola Light 134, 169
Coca-Cola Zero 68, 134, 169–70
Corus 133–4
Cuprinol 109–10
Cyber-shot 55

Brand name index 189

Dacia 3, 62, 66, 113–14
DAF Trucks 120–1
DanActive 65
Danone Actimel 65
Dell Computers 101, 106, 108, 113–14, 136
DHL 35
Diesel 113–14
DirectGov 123–4
Double A Paper 119–21
Dove 55, 67
DSM 33, 120
Dubai 122–3
Duracell 145
Dyneema 33
Dyson 30, 106–7

EasyJet 106, 136, 148
Edinburgh 123, 125
El Corte Ingles 135
Esso 154
Euro Shopper 110–11

Fairy 55
FedEx 119–21
Fina 154
First Choice Holidays 19
Flora 55, 67, 110
Florida 136
Formule 1 Hotels 115–17
Fysiq 64

General Motors 55
Geox 112–13
Gibson 112–13
Gillette Venus 68, 70
Giorgio Armani 33
Google 32, 38, 44, 116–17
Google Apps 121
Greenpeace 122
Grolsch 35
Groupe RCI Banque 3
GSUS 112
Gucci 145

H&M 33
Hallmark e-cards 116, 118
Harley-Davidson 63, 153
Harrods 115–16, 135–7, 151

Head & Shoulders 20, 55
Heineken 82, 109–10, 136
Heinz Baked Beans 110–11
Hertog Jan beer 109–10
Hewlett-Packard 32
Hitachi 55
HM Revenue and Customs 123, 125
Hong Kong 122–3
Hoover 105
HP 85, 102
HP. Invent 32
Huggies 143–4
Hyves 35

I4gotyourbirthday.co.uk 116, 118
Ibis Hotels 116, 118
ID&T 33–4
Impress 119
Infinit 101
Innocent Drinks 82, 134, 145–7, 150–1
Intel 101
Interpolis 36
iPhone 31
iPod 30–1, 102, 134
iTunes 102, 134

Jaguar 101
Jamie Oliver 6–7
Jetta 69
JVC 112–13

Kandoo 145
Kit Kat 108, 110–11
Kleenex 105
KLM Airlines 44
Knorr 67

Levi Strauss 53, 164–5
Lexus 101
LG 55
Lidl 106
Lipton 67
Lloyds 155
London Pass 123–4
L'Oréal 108, 110–11, 156
Lunn Poly 19
Lux 67
Lynx 55, 108

McDonald's 55, 82, 155
McKinsey & Company 119–20
Mama Cash 123, 125
Marlboro 2, 142
Marlies Dekkers 40
Mars 153
Mazda 113–14
MediaMarkt 106
Mercedes 101, 142
Merci 108
Michelin 77
Microsoft 113–14
Miele 112–13
Mini 66
Minute Maid 81, 134
Mona 59–60, 62–5, 134
Mosquito Festival, Clute, Texas 2
MP3 30, 134

Naked Chef 7
Nespresso 156, 171
Nestlé 53, 56, 109
Nestle Waters Direct 120–1
New York 107, 123–4
Nike 9, 26, 55, 149, 155
Nissan 3, 101
Nivea 52, 62, 69
Nokia 85, 108
North Rhine–Westphalia 122–3

Océ 21–3, 41, 45, 119–21
Office Christmas 119–21
OMO 159
O'Neill 113–14
One Percent Foundation 122–3
OpenSkies 53
Optimel 64, 134

PACCAR 120
Pampers 143–5
Passat 69
Pechiney 120
Pepsi-Cola 76, 169
Pepsi 7-Up Ice Cola 79
Phaeton 101
Philips 19, 53–4, 61, 136, 166
Philips Healthcare 119–21
Philishave 54
PlayStation 55

Porsche 165–6
PriceWaterhouseCoopers (PwC) 120
Pringles 20, 55, 62
Procter & Gamble 4–5, 19–20, 55, 109
Pullman 116, 118
PwC *see* PriceWaterhouseCoopers

Q8 154

Reckitt Benckiser 55
Renault 3, 12–13, 62, 66, 136
Repsol 154
Rexona 67
RijkZwaan 24
River Café 7
Rockwool 58
Rolls-Royce 66
Royal Canin 106
Royal Hoogovens 133–4
Royal Philips Electronics NV 53
Ryanair 106, 115–17

Salanova 24–5
Samsung 4, 55
Sara Lee 4, 109
Schiphol Airport, Amsterdam 104
Schmallbach-Lubeca 120
Scirocco 69
Seat 15
Sensation White 34
Senseo 113–14
Sensodyne 104
7-Up 141
7-Up Ice Cola 79
Shell 58, 154–5, 159–61
Signature 53
Singapore Airlines 136
Škoda 15, 106
Skype 102
Snack-a-Jacks 104
Sofitel 116, 118
Sony 4, 55, 101, 134
Southwest Airlines 28–30, 36, 44, 104
Special K Chocolately Delight 3
Starbucks 28, 37–9
Stella McCartney 33
Sun dishwashing tablet 83
Sunshine State 136
Super-Flex 143–4

Brand name index

Tamoil 154
Taurox 58
Tesco 33, 116–17
Texaco 154
The Leisure Pass Group 124
Thomson Holidays
Timotei 55
TNT 34–5, 48, 115–16
TomTom 105
Total 154
Toyota 26, 33, 55, 101
TripAdvisor 115–16
Tropicana 81–2, 134
TUI 19

Unilever 8, 30, 44, 55–7, 67, 111, 159, 167
United Airlines 28
UPC 35
US Airways 116, 118

Vaio 55
Vanish 111
Venus 68, 70
Vichy skincare 110–11
Vifit 59–60, 62–5, 134
Vincent van Gogh Museum 122–3
Virgin 27, 62, 77, 104, 115–16
Virgin Airways 30
Vital 52, 62, 69, 119–21
Vodafone 85
Volkswagen (VW) 15, 55, 69, 85, 101, 112–13
Volvo 12–13, 85, 87, 108, 136
V-Power 58, 159–61
VW *see* Volkswagen

Walkman 55, 101
Walmart 30
WeightWatchers 115–16
Werther's Original 110–11
WWF 155

Yakult 65
Yamaha 19, 55
Yamaha WaveRunner 55, 70
Yousendit.com 115–16

Zappos.com 115, 117